Praise for *A World of Wealth*

"An indispensable—and highly readable—primer on how the economic world really works, whether politicians of both left and right want it to work that way or not. If it were required reading for all political reporters, they might do a lot more reporting and carry a lot less water in the process."

—*John Steele Gordon*, Author of *Empire of Wealth: The Epic History of American Economic Power*

"Thomas Donlan reminds us all that capitalism is not simply one choice among different and equally valid economic systems, but instead that hard work and the accumulation of wealth is the natural tendency of successful people and healthy societies around the world."

—*Christopher Whalen*, Managing Director, Institutional Risk Analytics

"It has been several decades since Joseph Schumpeter observed that the philosophical defense of a free-market economy must never cease. Thomas Donlan has taken up that challenge, but this clear-eyed book is much more than a defense. It is a magnificently constructed explanation of how the world works and why free-market capitalism continues to offer the greatest hope for solving our greatest challenges."

—*Carl J. Schramm*, Ph.D., President, Kauffman Foundation

"Thomas Donlan's defense of free market capitalism is especially timely today given all the pressures to regulate and stifle it. The anti-globalization movement wants more trade protectionism and less immigration. The global credit crisis is putting pressure on governments to bail out irresponsible lenders and borrowers at taxpayers' expense. Instead, Donlan convincingly and clearly explains why we would all prosper more by doing all we can to make markets freer."

—*Ed Yardeni*, President, Yardeni Research, Inc.

"With the facts of a primer laid out in the fast-paced narrative of a storyteller, Thomas Donlan's *A World of Wealth* lucidly explains today's marketplace. From the credit crisis to immigration and from oil prices to global warming, the book guides the reader through the economic issues of our day—jargon-free. It's a fast, fun read that illuminates while it entertains."

—*Thomas W. Hazlett*, Professor of Law & Economics, George Mason University

"The author brings to the table a healthy skepticism of the conventional wisdom, an admirable ability to separate fact from fancy, and an undisguised repugnance for the mumbo-jumbo that's the curse of so much commentary on anything to do with economics or investment. *A World of Wealth* is not only a lively read, but an exceptionally enlightening and rewarding one to boot."

—*Alan Abelson*, *Barron's* Columnist

A WORLD OF WEALTH

A WORLD OF WEALTH

*How Capitalism Turns
Profits into Progress*

Thomas G. Donlan

Vice President, Publisher: Tim Moore
Associate Publisher and Director of Marketing: Amy Neidlinger
Executive Editor: Jim Boyd
Editorial Assistant: Pamela Boland
Development Editor: Russ Hall
Digital Marketing Manager: Julie Phifer
Marketing Coordinator: Megan Colvin
Cover Designer: John Barnett
Managing Editor: Gina Kanouse
Project Editor: Jovana San Nicolas-Shirley
Copy Editor: Betsy Harris
Proofreader: Meg Shaw
Senior Indexer: Cheryl Lenser
Compositor: Jake McFarland
Manufacturing Buyer: Dan Uhrig

© 2008 by Thomas G. Donlan
Published by Pearson Education, Inc.
Publishing as FT Press
Upper Saddle River, New Jersey 07458

FT Press offers excellent discounts on this book when ordered in quantity for bulk purchases or special sales. For more information, please contact U.S. Corporate and Government Sales, 1-800-382-3419, corpsales@pearsontechgroup.com. For sales outside the U.S., please contact International Sales at international@pearson.com.

Printed in the United States of America
First Printing: May 2008

ISBN-10: 0-13-235000-9
ISBN-13: 978-0-13-235000-6

Pearson Education LTD.
Pearson Education Australia PTY, Limited.
Pearson Education Singapore, Pte. Ltd.
Pearson Education North Asia, Ltd.
Pearson Education Canada, Ltd.
Pearson Educatión de Mexico, S.A. de C.V.
Pearson Education—Japan
Pearson Education Malaysia, Pte. Ltd.

Library of Congress Cataloging-in-Publication Data

Donlan, Thomas G.
  A world of wealth : how capitalism turns profits into progress / Thomas G. Donlan.
    p. cm.
  ISBN 0-13-235000-9 (hardback : alk. paper) 1. Capitalism—United States. 2. Free enter-
prise—United
States. I. Title.

  HB501.D654 2008
  330.973—dc22

                    2008003823

To Carol, who has heard it all before.

Contents

Acknowledgments

Like most writers, I stand on the shoulders of the giants who created the great economic ideas of the world. From that perch I have issued commentary and marginalia. I don't pretend to have had original thoughts about economics, but I hope I have clearly described a few economic truths.

I thank the economists, journalists, and editors who have informed and inspired me, especially Shlomo Maital, who first introduced me to the study of economics, and J. Stuart Hunter, the statistics professor whose marvelous lectures on a frightening subject somehow got me over my math phobia. I would never have encountered either of them without the generosity of the Sloan Foundation, which funded a fellowship for journalists to study economics at the Woodrow Wilson School of Public and International Affairs at Princeton University.

According to Dr. Samuel Johnson, the eighteenth-century British philosopher, scholar, and bon vivant, "No man but a blockhead ever wrote, except for money." I would like to thank my former editor, Alan Abelson; my editor, Ed Finn; my managing editor, Rich Rescigno; and our corporate parent, Dow Jones & Co., for paying me to write about economics in *Barron's National Business and Financial Weekly* these 25 years and more. Special thanks must go to Susan Witty, a copy editor at *Barron's* who carefully edited my editorials, especially those with which she most strongly disagreed. My colleague at *Barron's*, Washington Editor Jim McTague, provided a close review of the text at a crucial point. My wife, Carol Knopes Donlan, who is a far better editor than I deserve, also applied her skill to the project. None of these wonderful people are responsible for my views or the mistakes of fact or judgment that others may find.

This book, of course, does not contain everything known about economics, nor does it contain everything that a well-educated person or a good citizen should know about economics. It does offer, to the best of my ability, the inspiring truth of capitalism—which is that the study of money and wealth is above all the study of liberty.

—*Thomas G. Donlan*

About the Author

Thomas G. Donlan is Editorial Page Editor at *Barron's National Business and Financial Weekly* and has been writing about economics, business, and politics in his Editorial Commentary columns since 1992. He covered Washington for the magazine from 1981 to 1991. A graduate of Hamilton College and Indiana University, he attended Princeton University's Woodrow Wilson School of Public and International Affairs on a fellowship for journalists funded by the Sloan Foundation. He has written two other books on technology policy and on the decline of the private pension system. As a well-known writer on a wide variety of issues, he is often sought after for his opinions by major media.

Introduction

There are two kinds of economists: Those who think the free market always works, except when the results don't suit them; and those who think the free market never works, except when the results do suit them.

In my view, the free market always works. Whether the results suit me or you is a matter of taste, and if we don't like the results, we can change them anytime, just by adding our money to the market. The best thing about economics is the free market, and the best thing about the free market is freedom.

In this book, I am attempting to provide intelligible advocacy and explain economic issues, and I offer some historical background for the topics in each chapter.

I'm throwing out all the charts, graphs, and technical terms, throwing out the mathematical analysis, throwing out game theories, and throwing out professional economists. What remains is a way of looking at the world through the powerful lens of capitalist investment and productivity.

This book cannot give you all the answers, but I hope that after reading it, you will be ready to have interesting conversations with other intelligent people interested in politics, business, and history. If you take the lessons of this book to heart, you should be ready to have warm and vigorous conversations, for the ideas here are controversial. Many well-meaning people would rather impose their ideas on others for their own good; they recoil at the idea that people should make their own choices, for better or worse. The consistent philosophy in this book is that free markets are effective—capitalism provides superior solutions to most of our looming problems. Even more

A World of Wealth

important, free markets and capitalism are good because they promote individual liberty.

Economics has been called the "dismal science," and there's plenty going on in the world that supports that charge. Poverty and the unequal distribution of wealth, the population explosion, trade conflicts, immigration, outsourcing, environmental damage, rising energy prices, uncertain health and pension benefits, and many more discouraging economic issues push their way onto our computer displays, television screens, and front pages every day.

The phrase "dismal science" was coined by Thomas Carlyle, the nineteenth-century essayist, in a retort to the forecasts of Thomas Malthus, an economist who projected that the earth's food supply could not grow as fast as its population; hence, humanity is doomed to suffer frequent famines.

"Dreary, stolid, dismal, without hope for this world or the next," said Carlyle of the Malthusian prophecy. He also applied the whole phrase "dismal science" to his own economic argument in 1849 that freeing the slaves who worked the West Indies sugar plantations had not been in the slaves' best interests. Carlyle said that, without plantation owners' capital and enterprise, the best the former slaves could do on their own was subsistence agriculture and fishing. Sugar had been more lucrative and life as a slave had been more secure, he claimed.

Dismal science, indeed, if it were true. Man, however, does not live by bread alone: A hungry free man is better off than a well-fed slave. In this book, we explore some hard questions about capitalism and humanity. It's true that economics sometimes turns up some distressing conclusions because it is the science of human behavior stripped of all illusions. Economists observe what people do for money; it is often not a pleasant sight.

Capitalism is business, and the study of capitalism is the study of the sources and uses of profits—how money becomes wealth.

Although some historians consider capitalism to be a form of social organization, all forms of social organization are based on the concentration of wealth for investment, and societies prosper on the returns of their investments.

Studying capitalism should eventually produce an awakening like that of the Molière character who discovered he had been speaking prose all his life without knowing it. When we talk about the creation, distribution, and consumption of wealth, we are talking about capitalism, whether we believe in it or not.

Supply and demand are the chief forces in economics. Demand is always infinite and supply never is. We would all like to gorge ourselves on our favorite things, but they are not infinitely available. Prices are set by the availability of things—supply—and the combined desires of people to have certain things in preference to other things—demand. Supply and demand are hard to measure because they don't stand still. For each product or service in the global economy, supply and demand are constantly changing according to the needs and desires of billions of people. Large imbalances between supply and demand also occur, creating general price inflation or deflation. Economics theorists talk about "equilibrium," the point where supply and demand are in balance, prices are stable, and supplies are predictable. It is a wonderful mathematical exercise, worth many Nobel Memorial Prizes in Economic Science. But as Yogi Berra might have said, "The difference between theory and practice is that in theory, there is no difference, but in practice, there is." Any person interested in economics must understand that prices constantly change with the preferences of buyers and the availability of parts, labor, and capital (all of which also have prices set in markets).

Value is a different concept from price. There is no such thing as an intrinsic value of goods or services. Value in an economic sense is nothing but a price set in a market. It changes constantly.

Creating Capital

The origin of wealth lies in scarcity. Anything we can have without effort has no value. When we must work to hunt, mine, farm, when we buy tools and sell products, and when we must defend our gains, we establish an economy, an interrelationship of many people. As quickly, we become capitalists—owners of tools, large or small. Day laborers who own their shovels are in that small sense capitalists, just as owners of factories or farms are capitalists with more physical capital. We also work to acquire skills that can be termed human capital.

Goods and services are made and provided from ingredients, sometimes called the factors of production. The classic description of these ingredients is land, labor, and capital. Land is more than just a field—it stands for the resources of the earth, from mining to agriculture. Labor is more than the sweat of our brows—it stands for all forms of energy use. Capital is more than just money or wealth—it stands for tools, machinery, and knowledge.

Any product and nearly all services require judicious mixtures of all three, so management should be counted as a fourth factor of production. It is the human talent involved in combining the other three.

A farmer works the land using capital equipment, such as a plow, horse, or tractor, and seed. He is more productive if he knows how much seed is enough, how deeply to plow for the particular crop, how hard to work the horse, how much to feed him, and countless other variables. Even a peasant must manage complexity.

Available resources have changed over time as technology pushes the limits to growth. From horses to tractors, from seed gathered and saved to seed genetically engineered and sold at the farm dealer, from rain to irrigation, from manure to chemicals—every aspect of production changes because of technology.

Changes in social organization also affect the optimal allocation of land, labor, and capital. Sharecropping leaves little incentive to make permanent improvements; the growth of banking and credit make land more affordable; insurance and futures markets make ventures less risky; education makes farmers more skilled. The study of such forces may be the most serious, and certainly the most difficult, part of economics.

The 80-20 Rule

In any society, there will always be more followers than leaders, more losers than winners. An 80-20 rule seems to govern human affairs: Left to their own impulses, 80 percent of the work is done by 20 percent of the work force; 80 percent of property falls into the hands of 20 percent of the populace; 80 percent of the effort produces 20 percent of the value. Economists call it Pareto's Law, after Vilifredo Pareto, a nineteenth-century Italian economist who noticed 20 percent of Italians were earning 80 percent of the national income.

Here are some other examples of the 80-20 rule:

- Twenty percent of the devices, tools, and people on an assembly line are responsible for 80 percent of the defects.

- Twenty percent of the customers account for 80 percent of the profits. Also, 20 percent of the products and 20 percent of the sales force generate 80 percent of the profits.

- Twenty percent of the customers—a different 20 percent— also make 80 percent of the complaints.

- Workers who can schedule themselves—such as artists, writers, or senior office workers—get about 80 percent of their work done by working intensely about 20 percent of the time.

- Twenty percent of hospital patients and 20 percent of health insurance clients account for 80 percent of the costs of care.

Much derided and denounced, "trickle-down economics" refers to the concept that if the 20 percent who create wealth are left unfettered and lightly taxed, they and their investments will create more wealth, so the benefits will trickle down to the rest of society in the form of wages and profits. This should not be controversial; it should be taken as a fundamental principle of capitalism.

That's what it seemed like to Adam Smith, who noted that the wealthiest person cannot eat much more than anyone else. The rich man's food may be more artfully prepared, better decorated, served by a waiter in a fine uniform, or composed of more courses. Still, a meal is just a meal, and one can eat only so much.

In Smith's view, all the other trappings of wealth are conduits for trickle-down economics: If the wealthy diners were not wealthy, their chefs and sous-chefs might not be employed, their well-paid cake decorators might be baking cookies at home and selling them on the street, their waiters and the rest of their household staffs might be subsistence farmers. None of them could earn as much in such circumstances as they could on an eighteenth-century nobleman's estate. (That does not stop the servants from resenting their stations in life or from looking down on those not so well employed.)

Far more important but less visible, wealthy individuals invest their wealth in productive enterprises, which also employ factory workers, salespeople, executives, and janitors. Wealth does not merely trickle down—it gushes in cataracts and nourishes the entire society.

As Smith said of the rich, "They divide with the poor the produce of all their improvements."

In modern times, trickle-down economics burst upon the American political scene in the early days of the Reagan administration as a derogatory term for radical tax cuts, especially cuts in high progressive tax rates on high incomes. In 1981, the highest bracket of taxable income was taxed at 70 percent, although few people paid taxes at that rate because the tax code also offered many tax shelters.

Tax-cutters rarely dare to use the term trickle-down economics, although in one incident, President Reagan's budget director, David Stockman, privately conceded that his "supply-side economics" was really trickle-down economics, and the concession made it into a book that was published while the tax-cut controversy was still lively.

The debate was in two parts: Was it true that Republican tax-cutters wanted to cut rates on the rich? And was it true that cutting high tax rates on the rich would stimulate investment, create new jobs, and bring benefits to lower income classes?

Both things were true, although the effects take time to work their way through the economy, and other factors also operate. Some Democrats, however, believed trickle-down economics was a cruel hoax and the benefits for the middle class and the poor were nonexistent.

Republicans rarely come out well when Democrats accuse them of favoring the rich, and thus they rarely defend trickle-down economics well. They ignore it or run away from it as much as they can.

They should be casting the alternative in terms people can understand. The point of high tax rates is to take wealth away from individuals who have a lot of it, never mind that most of it is invested in the productive economy, where the returns on the investment are trickling down to everyone. Most government spending, however, is just spending—pure consumption that does little to create new wealth.

Democratic government has this fundamental problem: In broad terms, 20 percent of the people do most of the productive work and create most of the nation's wealth, but the other 80 percent command a heavy majority of votes. It's a pleasant surprise that democracies foster much investment and productivity growth at all.

The Power of Productivity

Economic productivity is something for every member of society to celebrate. When productivity is rising in a society, wealth is being created, and more and more wealth is available—through the trickle-down effect—to satisfy the wants and needs of the whole population. However a society chooses to divide its output, productivity drives output upward. There's nothing more important for the economic well-being of any society.

Labor productivity, however, is often misunderstood. It has little to do with how hard the work force labors. It actually measures the power of capital: Capitalists acquire the land necessary for their enterprise. Capitalists select the sources of the enterprise's raw materials. Capitalists borrow money or sell shares in the enterprise so they can make these investments and hire workers. (Or capitalists hire managers to do these things.)

When workers take their tools from the owner of the enterprise, use them according to the owner's direction, and become more productive than they could be on their own, their labor productivity increases. (Their labor productivity might also increase if they work harder each hour, if they bring their own, better tools to the factory, or if they acquire more training or education and learn to work smarter and more efficiently.)

Many economists separate out such intangible factors as advancing technology, innovation, managerial skill, luck, and organizational change and call these the fruits of total factor productivity, not of capital alone. Those who study this kind of productivity say that more than half the advancement of U.S. productivity since World War II has been the result of these intangible factors. But capitalists should get most of the credit for introducing new work methods as much as for purchasing new machinery.

For a simple example, suppose a furniture manufacturing business has been hiring skilled painters to brush-paint its products. The boss buys some paint sprayers, which are easier and faster to use. Almost immediately, the painters can paint 50 percent faster, with results that are just as good. Any student of productivity would consider this a case of capital deepening, in which the advancement of output is due to the increase of investment in capital equipment. Over time, the workers become more skilled with the new equipment, learning, for example, that they can layer several coats of paint without waiting for each coat to dry. The factory owner also rearranges the work floor so that the spray painters have easier access to the work they are painting. Output rises again, even though there was no further investment in capital equipment. This may be called an increase in total factor productivity, but it should be credited to the original capital investment in paint sprayers.

There are three ways a nation can enjoy more income, three ways to make the economic pie get bigger. First, more people can go to work: A country might encourage immigration to fill newly created jobs. Second, people can acquire more skills: A country might open educational opportunities to women, easing their entrance to highly paid professions. The United States has used both methods in recent decades, but they are not indefinitely repeatable opportunities. The third way is to encourage people to invest in plant, equipment, and organization. The third way is harder, more expensive, and potentially unlimited.

An important reason economics has been called the dismal science is that its honest practitioners offer so little comfort to politicians and other wishful thinkers. A dollar spent on ice cream won't be available later to spend on meat and potatoes. That's hard enough to accept, but here's something worse: Dollars spent on wages won't be available later for the business to purchase new equipment or build new factories, so later there will be fewer jobs, and fewer well-paying jobs, than there might have been had the boss paid less. Many of our leaders would prefer to tell us something else—that businesses can spend more money on wages and benefits and still have enough profits to create more jobs, or that corporate profits and individual capital gains can be cut or taxed without harming investment and productivity.

What is really dismal is that so many economists are ready to feed the fire of political redistribution. Reckless economists advise politicians to favor consumption over investment, labor over capital, and jam today over meat and potatoes and jam tomorrow.

The pursuit of productivity and wealth requires more self-restraint and more determined investment in the pursuit of profit. In the following chapters, we examine the continuing conflict between consumption and investment.

1

The Capitalist Answer to the "Energy Crisis": Pay Higher Prices

After years in the bottom drawer when oil prices were low, the economics of energy has returned to the top of the issues list. The difference between $20 oil and $100 oil concentrates public attention. But the highest price for energy may not be worse than the lowest price.

The United States should have an energy policy aimed at providing Americans with the greatest amount of energy at the least economic and social cost—in both the short run and the long run. How much we pay for gasoline at the pump is important; so is how much our grandchildren will pay for the energy they will need. How can we do both efficiently?

This is a fundamental economic question, not merely a question about energy.

Fortunately, the answer is quite simple: Every time we buy and use energy, we should pay a price that reflects the usefulness of the energy to all other possible customers—what they would pay for it. The price should also reflect the cost of creating the next bit of energy that will replace our bit in the market—which may be more or less than what it cost to produce our purchase.

The free market works at the intersection of demand and supply, at the intersection of the long run and the short run. Oil and other forms of energy move through the world propelled by companies and individuals. They are buying and selling, investing and speculating, profiting or losing when the price of energy goes up or down.

Think of the investments made to produce energy. Every year, the oil, gas, and coal industries spend many billions of dollars all over the world finding and developing new resources. Whether energy companies are owned by private shareholders or governments, they have one thing in mind: making money. They must make enough money to cover their costs, plus something to reinvest in expanding the business as demand for energy increases. It's all capitalism, though sometimes it works under assumed names.

Every year, the electric utilities of the world spend billions building and maintaining power plants and electric transmission lines. They spend many more billions buying fuel for the power plants. Their intention is simple: make money. The same is true for operators of oil tankers, makers of drilling equipment, creators of antipollution equipment, and all the other sectors and subsectors of the energy economy. They provide services for hire; in turn, they hire workers of all kinds, from roughnecks on the wells, to seamen on the ships, to geologists finding the next oil field.

As each of these participants in energy production finds a function and fills it, more cost is loaded into each barrel of oil, ton of coal, or megawatt-hour of electricity. When that energy is consumed—when work is done and products are made or services performed—money starts flowing back the other way from consumers to pay those costs. If the value of the work at the end of the line is great enough to cover the cost of extracting, refining, and delivering the energy to the user, a profit will probably occur at each stage of the production cycle.

Profits induce people to keep on doing what works. Making money, which to them means buying goods and hiring people for a little less than they make selling goods and services, is their reason for existence in business.

Losses can be even more important because they force people to avoid further failure, to try to do something different.

The use of energy is, or should be, a matter of using the tools of economics and engineering to help people live better. A high price for energy reduces demand by punishing waste. A low price does little to make people want to use energy frugally. Low prices tell consumers that all's well. But people can do more of what they want while using less energy, and high prices tell them that's what they should do. They can make investments that pay off environmentally and economically. Anyone who has put storm windows on a home or added insulation to an attic ceiling or house walls has seen a payoff from a conservation investment. The high cost of fuel changes the economics of operating a house; new investments may be needed. Saving fuel can be cheaper than buying fuel.

Nothing in capitalism demands that we waste resources or labor. Everything in capitalism insists that we produce at the lowest possible cost, all costs considered.

Market Movements

The price of oil is set on the world market by what sellers are willing to sell it for and what buyers are willing to pay for it. Prices go up and down with supply and demand. When they go up, companies book profits from selling inventories that were acquired cheaply. Shortsighted critics denounce these big profits, but producers must have the funds to buy the next round of supplies. If they make big profits, they have more money to find the next supplies.

Higher prices are the only realistic solution to high energy prices: High prices stimulate new supply, reduce demand, and signal the need for new energy technologies. Just within the realm of oil, the oil locked up in tar sands and oil shale in North America alone exceeds the reserves of the entire Middle East. They are not counted in reserves because it would cost too much to produce it. It could not be sold at a profit.

When the price of oil rises enough, the oil shale industry will get on its feet. Once it reaches a size where economies of scale take hold, the abundance of oil from the new supply will drive prices down. How can we know this is true? It happened years ago in Texas, the Gulf of Mexico, and even the Middle East. Each of those famously productive territories was once too speculative, too hard to reach, too far from markets, and too expensive to develop. Each time, and many other times, a shortage of production pushed prices up so much that the cost of developing a new oil patch came within reach. Each time, the new province of oil reserves brought so much new oil on the market that prices collapsed. After the railroads reached Texas oil country, after the offshore drilling rigs were built, and after the fleet of supertankers went into service, enormous quantities of oil had to be sold to pay for the investments.

The only times Americans have ever been inconvenienced by their reliance on imported oil were from 1974 to 1975 and 1978 to 1979, when the federal government intervened to save us from paying "too much" for oil and gave us energy shortages, with lines of cars around the block waiting to get into gas stations. As the nation should have learned in the noncrisis of 1990 to 1991 and the noncrisis of 2004 to 2008, real energy independence is the freedom to buy fuel on the market at a price reflecting the demand for the fuel, with as few distortions imposed by government as possible.

The Power of Price

When gasoline prices rise to $3 or more for a gallon of regular gas, American drivers may be forgiven for thinking there's a big problem. But the role of oil in the world economy is often overrated. Consider the size of the Saudi Arabian economy—45 percent of the desert nation's gross domestic product (GDP) consists of oil production. The whole Saudi economy produced only $286 billion in goods and services in 2005, much of it with the help of 5.5 million foreign workers. Taiwan, with about the same number of people and no oil resources to speak of, has a GDP twice as big.

Energy is one input—it does not determine the fate of a whole economy.

Until 1973, energy consumption rose in lockstep with GDP for most industrial nations. That was the easy way to grow. Thanks to cheap oil, energy was the least costly of common economic inputs. Using more energy was the cheapest path to a more profitable product.

Sudden increases in the price of oil in the 1970s broke the relationship between energy and output—much to the surprise of many energy economists. The world adapted, gradually but thoroughly. At first, high prices summoned geologists and engineers to find new supply sources; later the abolition of price controls in the U.S. rearranged the economics of oil in the ground. The U.S. could import more cheap foreign oil and avoid being forced to exploit expensive domestic oil.

Oil actually proved to be abundant, and many nations—Mexico, Norway, the United Kingdom, Indonesia, Russia, Venezuela, and Nigeria, to name a few important ones—had a lot of it. The price of oil fell.

Perhaps surprisingly, the supply of oil did not fall with the price. Oil exporters were as willing to supply it at low prices as they were at high prices at the peak of the 1970s energy bubble. They had oil, and they had invested in production facilities. They could not eat oil. They couldn't afford not to sell it. They had to take the price set in the market. The most they could do was stop investing in new production facilities, and some oil-producing countries could not even do that because they needed oil revenues to purchase goods their own weak economies could not produce.

The Organization of Petroleum Exporting Countries (OPEC), the so-called oil cartel, had little if any power to punish cheating members, limit the production of nonmembers, or restrict the world supply in some other way. Member countries pursued their own self-interests, not caring if fellow members said they were "cheating" by producing too much.

In economists' terms, the price of oil is driven by demand in the short term, and demand was generally weaker than supply from about 1982 to 2003.

Other factors of production became more important than energy because energy was cheap–almost as low as $10 a barrel as recently as 1998. In the 1980s and 1990s, when oil prices were low, the most profitable way to increase productivity was to rearrange labor costs. Japanese firms moved factories to the U.S., Korea, Taiwan, and China; Europeans moved factories to the U.S. and to Eastern Europe. The U.S. moved production to Mexico and then to China and elsewhere in Asia, and it loosened its immigration restrictions, formally and informally, to find workers for the new jobs being created.

European and Japanese industrialists moved to the U.S. to take advantage of the world's most capital-intensive and productive labor force, and they moved to Central Europe and Asia seeking cheaper workers. American industrialists moved their less-productive jobs overseas, in part because the foreigners were bidding up American labor costs and in part because there weren't enough new people to fill all the old and new jobs.

The "giant sucking sound" made famous by Ross Perot was actually the sound of a giant valve operating to relieve the pressure of too many jobs chasing too few workers. If freer trade with Mexico had really been bad for America as Perot imagined, it would have produced higher unemployment in the U.S. Jobs were lost but others were created, more than offsetting the losses.

In the past few years, however, the price of energy has been rising, especially in terms of the falling U.S. dollar. It's a demand-driven price again, in a world economy that has expanded faster than expected.

The Limits of Planning

As the price of oil rises and falls, it drives businessmen to the edge of sanity and politicians well beyond the edge. How can anyone plan for the future if we can't predict the price of one of the most important resources that drives national progress, national income, and national wealth?

Fortunately, planning is part of the problem, not the solution. For about 30 years, economists and politicians have been flirting with a variety of national energy policies, most of them at least slightly crazy. They have tried inflation, price controls, supply allocations, supply subsidies, demand suppression, taxes, tax credits, regulation, and deregulation, and they have—most unforgettably—declared that the whole enterprise was "the moral equivalent of war," an idea appropriately known by its acronym, "MEOW."

Every president since Nixon has tried to impose a national energy policy, with or without a czar, and every president has failed. The reason: A national energy policy is impossible. Only a free market can send useful signals to suppliers and consumers, forcing them to make the difficult choices about their use of resources or to invent unexpected solutions that increase efficiency.

Remember these bold words?

"We will break the back of the energy crisis; we will lay the foundation for our future capacity to meet America's energy needs from America's own resources." That's what Richard M. Nixon said in his State of the Union speech during the Arab oil embargo in January

1974. He went on, "Let this be our national goal: At the end of this decade, in the year 1980, the United States will not be dependent on any other country for the energy we need to provide our jobs, to heat our homes, and to keep our transportation moving." Nixon's chief accomplishment was to impose price controls on oil and natural gas, an essential element in the ignition of a cycle of inflation and recession that lasted more than a decade.

The year after that speech, with the economy still reeling from the high price of energy, a new president resolved that the United States should be energy-independent and even be able to export energy again: "To make the United States invulnerable to foreign disruption, I propose standby emergency legislation and a strategic storage program of 1 billion barrels of oil for domestic needs and 300 million barrels for national-defense purposes. I will ask for the funds needed for energy research and development activities. I have established a goal of 1 million barrels of synthetic fuels and shale oil production per day by 1985, together with an incentive program to achieve it. Within the next 10 years, my program envisions 200 major nuclear power plants, 250 major new coal mines, 150 major coal-fired power plants, 30 major new refineries, 20 major new synthetic fuel plants, the drilling of many thousands of new oil wells, the insulation of 18 million homes, and the manufacturing and the sale of millions of new automobiles, trucks, and buses that use much less fuel."

That was Gerald R. Ford's program in 1975. The Strategic Petroleum Reserve was a relatively successful part of the program in the sense that it actually exists, though it's smaller today than what Ford imagined in 1975. Corporate Average Fuel Economy standards also exist. The less said about either one, the better. Higher fuel prices could have done more with less fuss, but most American politicians prefer low prices, an elaborate bureaucracy, and a continual fight among themselves to adjust the fuel-economy standards.

Most of Ford's other plans vaporized. Although candidates and presidents cribbed from his list of priorities for the rest of his life,

Ford's vision of energy independence was considerably farther out of reach in 2007 than it was in 1975.

Determined to be more effective, the next president declared the struggle for energy independence to be the "moral equivalent of war." Unfortunately, Jimmy Carter declared the war on the U.S. economy, creating the Department of Energy and winning the enactment of a comprehensive national energy policy. He also pushed Congress to pass Ford's idea of a windfall-profits tax, depriving energy companies of money they could have used to enlarge and modernize their industry. He created subsidies for energy conservation, solar energy, wind energy, gasohol, synthetic fuels to be made from coal, and the trans-Alaska pipeline, distorting energy markets and leaving American citizens and businesses feeling that energy efficiency was a government entitlement program.

Offsetting these missteps was the great achievement of the Carter administration in energy: Congress enacted laws to end Nixon's price controls on oil and natural gas.

The next president hardly needed an energy policy. Ronald Reagan needed only to confirm the decontrol of oil and natural-gas prices, watch freedom take effect, and stand aside as high prices called forth more supply around the world. The U.S. diversified its purchases of imported oil and conserved its own resources. Buying from low-cost producers was far more efficient than subsidizing high-cost domestic drillers.

Reagan gave eight State of the Union speeches and mentioned energy only twice—once to herald complete decontrol of energy prices and once to request demolition of the Department of Energy. During his presidency, the inflation-adjusted price of oil and other forms of energy nearly collapsed.

This was not entirely good news: High prices had made most sectors of the economy more energy efficient. The American economy enjoyed higher productivity for years after, partly because of its increased energy efficiency, but low prices sapped the will to invest still more in efficiency.

The latest national energy policy was enacted in 2005, and even President Bush acknowledged as he signed the bill that it would be a first step: "This bill is not going to solve our energy challenges overnight. Most of the serious problems, such as high gasoline costs or the rising dependence on foreign oil, have developed over decades. It's going to take years of focused effort to alleviate those problems."

There is, however, very little focus in the national Energy Policy Act. It sets self-contradictory goals, as it must if it seeks lower gasoline prices and reduced dependence on foreign oil. One or the other may be possible, but most of the oil that's cheap to produce comes from overseas, and all the possible domestic substitutes are expensive.

The 2005 Energy Policy Act promotes conservation and greater exploitation of existing fuel resources. It favors coal and nuclear energy. It seeks greater production of oil and natural gas and rejects development of offshore resources in Alaska, California, and the Florida Gulf Coast. It pays for research into oil production from tar sands and oil shale and for renewable energy substitutes such as wind, ethanol, and biodiesel.

In the America of the newest National Energy Policy, the government likes and supports some things, and it doesn't like and tries to suppress other things.

The government likes oil drillers and refiners and substitute forms of petroleum and natural gas. All are worthy of subsidies, even though the market is providing generous incentives already, in the form of high prices. It likes farmers, too—its favorite substitute for oil is ethanol from corn, which receives generous subsidies for producers and processors. Subsidies also flow to diesel fuel made wholly or in part from vegetable oil. Both ethanol and biodiesel cost about a dollar more than their oil-based competitors, but the National Energy Policy subsidizes the market for them and mandates that refiners provide them.

The government likes coal but wishes it weren't so dirty to burn, so it will pay for more research into ways of making "clean coal." Some day, if all goes better than it ever has, the government will build a coal-fired electric generating plant that has no more harmful emissions than an atomic power plant. While we are waiting, it is also going to subsidize the construction of nuclear power plants and subsidize insurance for them.

The government likes imported liquid natural gas (LNG), and Congress isn't going to let any not-in-my-backyard neighbors get in the way: The Federal Energy Regulatory Commission will have exclusive jurisdiction to decide where LNG shipping terminals can be built and new electric transmission lines will receive the same treatment. But there is no federal override of state and local authority over the location of new power plants, especially not for locating new nuclear power plants. The government likes them, but not that much.

The government likes energy efficiency at home, so it gave a 10 percent tax credit to homeowners for investing in saving energy—but only in 2006 and 2007 and only for investments up to $5,000, only $2,000 of which can be for improving windows.

The government dislikes appliances that use too much energy, so there are new efficiency standards for refrigerators, ceiling fans, torchiere lights, and space heaters. The government doesn't like to make us pay the full value of efficient appliances, so it gives us tax credits to offset the cost of improving home-energy efficiency through the purchase of better central air conditioners, water heaters, storm windows, insulation thermostats, and other equipment. Some of these attract 30 percent tax credits; some don't. Some were for 2006 and 2007 only, and some lasted longer. The government likes accountants and tax lawyers even more than it likes energy efficiency.

The government doesn't like restraints on the use of inefficient automobiles; it will not mandate that car engines be inspected for efficient operation, which would save energy and clean the air at the same time. Nor will it raise any fuel taxes. It thinks conservation and efficiency can go too far by making people pay a lot.

The government does like efficient automobiles, really it does, but it knows we don't like to pay for them, so we get tax credits to help us buy diesel cars, fuel-cell cars, electric-gasoline hybrid cars, and cars that can use more ethanol. But not too much: The tax credits are capped at $3,400 per vehicle, and they are reduced for vehicles that are successful in the market. The credits are phased out for any model that sells more than 60,000 units. That's because the government likes American car companies, which are unlikely to sell as many favored cars as Toyota and Honda.

As this brief sample of our government's energy likes and dislikes makes all too clear, what the government really likes is wishful thinking, and what it really doesn't like is taking the heat for higher prices. The government isn't sure if it likes profits or not and it doesn't understand the role they play in the market. But higher prices and bigger profits are what we need if we want to use energy more wisely.

Doing the Right Thing in Spite of Ourselves

While H.L. Mencken probably had it right when he said nobody ever went broke underestimating the intelligence of the American public, it is also true that Americans are capable of learning from their mistakes. Winston Churchill observed that, after trying everything else, Americans will usually do the right thing.

That's why we aren't in long lines on odd-numbered days, waiting for dwindling supplies of gasoline to be delivered—whatever is left after adequate supplies are rationed out to anyone the government considers an essential user. We tried that twice in the 1970s, and it didn't work either time.

Americans learned that a freely floating price clears a market and matches demand with supply. They have learned that price controls—on gasoline, anyway, if not on pharmaceuticals or city rents—are self-defeating and lead to shortages, rationing, more shortages, and general annoyance.

Most American politicians have been careful not to mention price controls on gasoline, even as oil and refined products set record price after record price in dollar terms. (Adjusted for inflation, the $39.50-a-barrel oil-price record set in 1980 is equivalent to about $90 a barrel today.)

We could be doing a lot to create more supply. We could, for example, open the Alaska National Wildlife Refuge for exploratory drilling. There may be oil there. The drilling site is a tiny portion of a barren plain, but there are those who love it, and they have friends in high places who are every bit as powerful as the friends of the energy industry.

Drilling there should be allowed, just as it should be allowed in the waters off the west coast of Florida, the Santa Barbara Channel, and other politically sensitive areas. Environmental damage can be prevented, controlled, and punished without invoking prior restraint. But advocates of new drilling on the Arctic coastal plain, Florida, and California don't have the votes in the U.S. Senate. They can console themselves with the thought that the oil won't evaporate, and if it's ever really needed, it will still be there, caribou or no caribou. New wells in Alaska couldn't affect the world price of oil for at least a decade, anyway.

The best thing Congress could do, however, is get out of the energy business and eliminate the Department of Energy in the bargain. Most of what the federal government does in the energy industry involves subsidies, tax breaks, and targeted investments.

Economically useful actions could be done privately without federal intervention, but private interests are waiting to see if free money falls from the sky before committing their own resources.

One of the most curious oversights in the quest for clean energy sources is nuclear power. The U.S. has 103 nuclear power plants, generating about 20 percent of American electricity needs. But no plants have been ordered since the accident at the Three Mile Island plant in 1979. No accidents have occurred in the U.S. since 1979, and even that accident did not kill or sicken anyone. Dozens of people die every year in U.S. coal-mine accidents, hundreds are injured, and hundreds more suffer before death from black-lung disease, but American utilities have ordered many big coal-fired power plants since 1979.

The explanation is that many people are afraid of nuclear power. They associate nuclear fission with the bombs that so shockingly destroyed Hiroshima and Nagasaki at the end of World War II. They don't understand the science and engineering that makes nuclear power generation different from atomic bomb-making, and they have little faith in those who tell them it's safe. The 1979 accident at Three Mile Island, which was dangerous but caused no serious damage to anything but the reactor, took its toll on public trust in nuclear power. The deadly Soviet accident at Chernobyl in 1986 was even more shattering. Unfortunately, some wild estimates of deaths and long-term damage were current in the news at the time and never reduced in the public mind to reflect reality.

There are two big technical issues that are serious: the disposal of spent fuel, which is dangerously radioactive but no longer useful for generating power, and the protection of all sorts of nuclear material, fuel, spent fuel, and by-products. If the wrong people obtained it, some of the material could be used to make weapons. It's also true that nuclear power plants operated with bad intent could be used to enrich fuel to the concentrations needed to make atomic bombs.

This last danger should not create an objection for U.S. power plants; we should be able to police and regulate them in our own country. Protecting nuclear material and spent fuel isn't that hard either, but we get in our own way doing it.

Since the 1970s, the United States has declined to reprocess spent nuclear fuel. President Carter decided it set a bad example for the world because reprocessing plants present the easiest opportunities to create bomb-grade nuclear fuel. Carter decided that if we don't want other countries to reprocess fuel, we should not do it ourselves. Unfortunately, the rest of the world did not follow our example. Reprocessing plants operate in Russia, France, and Japan; China and India have plans to build them.

The American choice for dealing with spent nuclear fuel has been to bury it at a specially equipped cavern in Nevada. The Yucca Flats facility has been fought over for decades. If it's ready at last in 2010, as now expected, it will have only the capacity to store the spent nuclear fuel already created, which is currently stored at the nation's existing nuclear power plants. It will not be available as a repository for future waste created after 2010. For that, the country will have to enlarge Yucca Flats or build another repository—and argue about it for another couple decades.

Recycling through reprocessing makes more sense than just burying spent nuclear fuel rods. The quantity of dangerous waste would be substantially reduced, and the amount of energy extracted from a given quantity of uranium ore would be substantially increased. It's a more efficient solution.

Nuclear power plants do have to be built correctly, by experts, and there is a need for close scrutiny—independent regulation of construction—by a team of other experts. In the U.S., we have depended on the Nuclear Regulatory Commission to watch the electric companies and their construction contractors.

Problems have occurred, but no big mistakes. Still, the federal regulators can't be everywhere and can't do everything. That, however, was the assumption during the Eisenhower administration, which worked with Congress to eliminate the normal private sector approach to dangerous projects in favor of government regulation. Fearing that no American electric company would venture into the unknown world of nuclear power generation, the Eisenhower administration and Congress sharply limited the utilities' potential liability for damages caused by nuclear power plant accidents.

This relieved the utilities of the necessity of paying huge sums for insurance premiums and relieved insurance companies of the responsibility for evaluating the safety of power plants. All the responsibility was put on the Nuclear Regulatory Commission (NRC), then known as the Atomic Energy Commission.

As a general rule, bureaucrats have no incentive to make a success out of what they regulate, although they have huge incentives not to let it become a failure. NRC regulation has been heavy-handed and slow, not merely risk-averse but averse to making any kind of decision without endless study. It earns no premiums for doing a careful but quick evaluation and pays no penalty for doing it inefficiently.

Federal regulation may have been an appropriate regime for the 1950s, when nuclear technology was new and a closely guarded military secret. Only a federal regulator could handle the knowledge that would supply the weapons for World War III. But if it remains appropriate decades later, it is hard to see why. Countries as technologically backward as Pakistan and North Korea have mastered bomb-making engineering; 30 countries operate 439 power plants; 69 countries operate nuclear reactors for research.

The civilian nuclear power industry is beginning to recover from the long shock that followed Three Mile Island. In 2007, the NRC received its first full application to build a new nuclear power plant since 1978, and there are dozens of preliminary filings from utilities testing the regulatory waters.

Are We Really Running Out of Oil?

In 1956, geologist M. King Hubbert predicted that the U.S. would hit peak oil production in 1970. He was right, at least for the time being. No matter how fast wildcatters have found new reserves or producers have drilled wells in the U.S., new supplies have not off-set declining production from older wells.

Hubbert died in 1989 but his followers now make the same pre-diction about world oil production: Between 2004 and 2030, the world has reached, or will reach, the peak, and no amount of furious search-ing will ever replace all the wells that are running dry. So they say.

There's a lesson here, but not the one oil prognosticators offer. The correct lesson is to not ask geologists about economics. Hubbert's prophecy holds only as long as the price of oil defines the supply.

We have no idea how much oil is still to be found. What we do know is that the more oil prices rise, the more oil will be produced. Furthermore, the more oil that is produced, the more likely it is that prices will fall.

A quick look around the world finds uneconomic oil in many places. Venezuela has more oil than Saudi Arabia, if you count its ultra heavy crude and tar sands. Canada has more than Saudi Arabia, if you count its tar sands. The U.S. has more than Saudi Arabia many times over, if you count its oil shale and coal, which could be con-verted to gasoline and diesel fuel.

Price is the problem, not geology. At the $20-per-barrel average market price (adjusted for inflation) that has prevailed for decades and has determined what oil can be produced at a long-term profit, tar sands, oil shale, and coal conversion have not looked like good investments. It costs too much to build the extraction industry and rebuild the refining industry, so these resources aren't counted as reserves.

As noted earlier, however, once upon a time it cost too much to drill in a far-off desert and build a fleet of supertankers to carry the oil to customers. Once upon a time it cost too much to drill offshore and build underwater pipelines to carry the oil to customers. Once upon a time it cost too much to pump more than about a third of the oil from any given well. Then, when some critical oil field in Pennsylvania or Texas reached peak production and market prices rose, the required investments suddenly made sense.

Once the industry adapted to the new definition of producible oil, the new supplies supported by new infrastructure overwhelmed the market, and the price fell back to that inflation-adjusted average of about $20.

We should be nearly certain that the process of boom and bust will prevail at least once more. Oil at $100 means oil at $20 eventually, even if it has to go higher to get there.

If world oil production peaks soon, it is quite possible that there will be problems. The world might need two decades for a crash program to develop new liquid-fuel sources. The U.S. Department of Energy estimates construction of a single substitute-fuel plant could cost $5 billion and require the better part of a decade to build. Such a plant might yield 100,000 barrels of liquid fuels per day—a drop in the world's energy bucket if a world oil shortage quickly escalated to tens of millions of barrels per day.

But build we must, say many of the worriers, stressing their view that the market cannot create new sources of energy in time to avert an economic crisis. Whether their favorite is a hydrogen economy or the creation of synthetic fuels, they call for government investment and government subsidy to bring the price of alternatives within reach of the marketplace.

It's a big job, calling for a big government with big ideas—just the kind of government we should have learned not to trust. The pathetic excuse for an energy bill pending in Congress is replete with special subsidies and attempts to manage the future.

Energy is traded in markets, and markets mitigate the economic impact with price increases. There will never be a serious long-term shortage of energy as long as we do not impose price controls or impose a political vision of new fuels and technologies.

There will just be higher prices, and some uses of oil will be priced out of the market. This will be no disaster: All users of energy will be forced to conserve it. At the same time, price increases will drive capital and capitalists toward newly attractive investment opportunities in energy supplies, just as low prices drove investors away from the oil business for the last two decades.

Profits are the appropriate spur to timely action. Government energy "investments" made before profits can be earned in the market are just welfare programs for geologists and engineers.

The messy, chaotic mechanisms of the market, which nobody can predict or control, offer the safest and most efficient routes to energy security. We won't have to fight the Chinese or the Indians for energy; we will have to use energy and other economic inputs more efficiently to stay rich enough to afford all the energy we need.

Peak Coal Foreshadowed Peak Oil

In 1865, an English economist of similar mind anticipated peak-oil geologist M. King Hubbert. William Stanley Jevons contemplated the exhaustion of British coal supplies, which then seemed inexhaustible. After a discussion of rising consumption and fixed supply that drew heavily on the methods of Thomas Malthus, Jevons then rejected other sources of energy, such as firewood, water power, tidal energy, windmills, and electricity. In a book titled *The Coal Question*, he said, "Petroleum has of late years become the matter of a most extensive trade, and has even been proposed by American inventors for use in marine steam-engine boilers. It is undoubtedly superior to coal for many purposes, and is capable of replacing it. But then, what is petroleum but the essence of coal, distilled from it by terrestrial or artificial heat? Its natural supply is far more limited and uncertain than that of coal, its price is about 15 pounds per ton already, and an artificial supply can only be had by the distillation of some kind of coal at considerable cost. To extend the use of petroleum, then, is only a new way of pushing the consumption of coal. It is more likely to be an aggravation of the drain than a remedy." Putting an end to the discussion, Jevons concluded, "We must not dwell in such a fool's paradise as to imagine we can do without coal what we do with it."

Jevons had limited understanding of geology and chemistry as applied to petroleum, and he also had limited insight into the power of prices. That 15-pound-per-ton price for petroleum was already inspiring new discoveries and new technology for exploitation. The inflation-adjusted price of petroleum, indeed, would never again be so high.

For many years after Jevons, British prosperity was indeed founded on coal-fired steam power. By the 1960s, however, his forecast that coal production would be played out had nearly come true. Many British mines produced nothing but rock, others only very low-grade coal. By that time, however, the coal mines of Britain were under the control of the state, and the state was in thrall to the national miners' union. A courageous and practical prime minister, Margaret Thatcher, closed unproductive mines and accepted the inevitable strike. It turned out that imported coal, oil, and gas were competitive with British coal. The miners lost their rock-digging jobs but the nation went forward, more productive, better fueled, and less beholden to its overprivileged unions.

Summary

Twice in recent years the high cost of energy has focused Americans' attention on economic principles. They have learned that supply and demand push and pull markets and that they work better when governments don't interfere very much. The massive inconveniences of long gas lines in the 1970s were the fault of government price controls and supply allocations. By the beginning of 2008, Americans were facing higher prices than in 1979, adjusted for inflation, and yet there were no gas lines because markets were allowed to function.

Likewise, the goal of energy independence is chimerical. We already have access to the sources of energy in the world energy market, where prices reflect the current need for fuel, the world's best estimate of future demand, and the world's best estimate of the marginal cost of replacing a unit of energy with a new one. These are the lowest possible realistic prices at the moment.

Finally, high prices will do more in less time to cure a shortage of energy than anything else. High prices will curtail use, focus consumers on using energy efficiently, and create the capital necessary for investment in new sources of energy. If we let the market decide which sources of energy best satisfy our needs, we will have what we need at the lowest possible cost.

2

The Capitalist Approach to Environmental Pollution and Global Warming: Breathe Easy

Over the eons, Earth has been much colder and much warmer than it is now, without human help or hindrance. Over the past 12,000 years, the planet has generally been warming, removing such natural features as the glaciers that covered the upper Midwest of what is now the United States. It seems to be a truth that the process is continuing, probably hastened by carbon dioxide emitted by the furnaces and machines of man.

How much warming is from increased carbon dioxide, rather than other causes, and how much of the carbon-dioxide increase is from nonhuman sources, such as volcanoes? How erratic has the warming process been? Such physical questions have been put to climatologists, paleontologists, and geologists, who have delivered a variety of responses adding up to "some."

The Intergovernmental Panel on Climate Change (IPCC), a United Nations organization, assesses and summarizes what scientists know about climate change. For work analyzing and publicizing climate change, the panel shared the 2007 Nobel Peace Prize with former Vice President Al Gore. As of 2007, the IPCC said it is "unequivocal" that warming is occurring and almost as certain that it is significantly forced by emissions of carbon dioxide from combustion in humankind's machines. The report still leaves a lot of room for further research. And there are scientists on each far-out end of the bell curve of opinion: Some say it's all overblown while others say the IPCC is far too cautious about an impending global disaster.

It may have been Cardinal Richelieu, the advisor to King Louis XIII of France, who first gave this advice about making predictions: "When you give a date, don't give a number, or when you give a number, don't give a date." It's good advice for any forecaster, and it's advice Al Gore seems to have taken to heart when he constructed his Nobel Peace Prize-winning global warming crusade.

In *An Inconvenient Truth*, the Oscar-winning movie of a lecture Gore delivered to many audiences, the former vice president warns of potential sea-level changes of 20 feet while showing slides of people in water up to their eyeballs in New Orleans—a hurricane disaster that had nothing to do with rising sea level. His critics consider this a falsehood; his allies consider it a dramatic illustration of something almost inevitable that hasn't actually happened yet. The IPCC's worst-case estimate, however, projects an increase in sea level of less than three feet by the end of the twenty-first century. Big changes in sea level are improbable unless global warming goes on for millennia, the 2007 report said. Some of the same people who take the IPCC's reports as proof that man-made global warming exists refuse to accept the IPCC's failure to forecast an imminent disaster.

True, changing the sea level by 20 feet would put a lot of people in deep water and, indeed, redraw the map of the world. Just in the U.S., it would shrink Florida, immerse a lot of waterfront property along all the coasts, and force the expenditure of many billions of dollars to erect Dutch-style flood barriers to keep the ocean out of coastal cities. Worldwide, some islands would disappear; some estuaries would flood. Certainly tens of millions of people would have to protect themselves or move. It is also certain that moving them or protecting them would be expensive.

Expensive? Global warming is not just an environmental problem; it is also an economic problem. Treating global warming as an environmental problem, we would ask physical scientists how much the sea might rise and how quickly. Treating it as an economic problem, we would try to figure out our most efficient response—not only to the most likely event, whatever the physical scientists conclude that may be, but also to the less likely outcomes, just in case the physical scientists miscalculate.

As a potential cause of a 20-foot rise in sea level, Gore offers rapid melting of the Greenland and Antarctic ice caps. But he doesn't give a date. The IPCC's 2007 report said that at the present rate of warming, the Greenland ice cap is not likely to melt for thousands of years, and that the Antarctic ice cap would probably grow, not melt, because there would be increased snowfall. Should we spend money to avoid such an unlikely disaster? How much should we spend? These are economic questions.

Many environmentalists are determined to freeze carbon-dioxide emissions as quickly as possible. Some, including Gore, say the world should also aim to reduce carbon emissions by 90 percent by 2050. How could we do that? Among the most commonly heard ideas is that all nations should comply with the Kyoto Accord, which committed nations to try to reduce their carbon-dioxide emissions, and then the world community should sprint to negotiate and ratify a new, tougher treaty that would take effect in 2010 and limit carbon-dioxide emissions. The problem with this is that most nations that have signed the Kyoto Accord have not lived up to their commitments. Also, the largest emitter of carbon dioxide—the United States—refused to sign. So did the two nations whose emissions are growing the fastest, China and India.

Meeting the Kyoto Accord goals, and certainly going beyond them, would require nations to choose one of two paths: impose taxes on carbon-dioxide emissions or impose strict limits on carbon-dioxide emissions.

A third way combines these but leaves more room for adjustment: after imposing both taxes and limits, allow emissions permits to be traded among large users of fossil fuel so that those who can reduce their emissions most cheaply will sell permits to those who face high costs.

This is commonly referred to by the shorthand term "cap and trade." It would create a market for evaluating the right to emit carbon dioxide, but it would be a market for certificates issued by countries or a world carbon-dioxide commission.

This solution may turn out to be one of those markets that works in theory but has problems in practice. Such a market, under the control of a government authority, would be vulnerable to changes in the supply of carbon-emission certificates. Such market manipulation might be well-meaning, but all too likely to end in favoritism and corruption. One need only look at the business tax systems in any country—laced with favors, subsidies, and attempts at behavior modification—to have an idea of the kind of inefficient complexity that would be the biggest threat to good results from such a system.

Shrinking the Energy Budget

If the world is to reduce its emissions of carbon dioxide by 90 percent, the U.S.—the biggest and most technologically advanced emitter—will gradually eliminate all activity fueled with coal, oil, and natural gas, unless those sources of energy could be engineered to emit virtually no carbon dioxide, or unless a great deal of carbon dioxide could be extracted from the air and stored to offset new emissions. Otherwise, the country would have only as much material production as can be managed with electricity generated in hydroelectric dams, nuclear plants, and alternative energy, such as wind generators and solar power.

Gore says this "really shouldn't be seen as a partisan issue or even a political issue. It's a moral issue."

It should be seen as an economic issue. Achieving such goals will take an extraordinary redeployment of American energy production. In 2006, this was the distribution of the U.S. energy budget by source, according to the U.S. Department of Energy:

- Coal, 22.5 percent

- Natural gas, 22.4 percent

- Oil, 39.8 percent

- Nuclear, 8.2 percent

- Hydroelectric dams and renewables, 6.8 percent
  (See *Annual Energy Review 2006*, Tables 1.3 and 2.1b-2.1f, and 10.3, published by the Energy Information Administration. Shares don't add up to 100 percent because of independent rounding.)

Fossil fuels, which are the primary sources of carbon-dioxide emissions, accounted for more than 84 percent of the energy consumed in the U.S. in 2006, which amounted to just under 100 quadrillion British Thermal Units (BTUs, a measure of heat that equalizes statistics about different forms of energy). Replacing that much combustion, or cleansing it of carbon dioxide, is a daunting enough task, but it's worse than that: Mere replacement allows no room for economic growth without offsetting improvements in energy efficiency.

The United States has already improved its energy efficiency dramatically. In 1970, the country consumed 18,000 BTUs of energy to produce a dollar of GDP (adjusted for inflation, using year-2000 dollars), whereas in 2006 it consumed less than 9,000 BTUs for each dollar of GDP. Partly because energy use was managed well and became more efficient, economic output in those 36 years grew from

$3.8 trillion of GDP to $11.4 trillion (also adjusted for inflation using year-2000 dollars.) Even though the energy cost of a dollar of economic output fell 50 percent, energy use rose from 67 quadrillion BTUs to 99 quadrillion BTUs because economic output nearly tripled.

In purely economic terms, this is a problem that other countries would like to have. China, for example, produces about one-tenth as much GDP as the United States and uses nearly as much energy as the United States in doing it. In environmental terms, however, it indicates that the carbon-dioxide emission challenge is insoluble with the technology we have. The more efficient we become, the more we can grow; the more we grow, the more we emit, despite increased efficiency.

With current technology, only deliberate reductions in economic growth can deliver the environmental benefits we would like to achieve from energy efficiency. Without a major change in technology, neither the United States nor any other country can expect to maintain its economic output after doing its fair share to cut fossil-fuel emissions by 90 percent. Much less can the world increase its output to satisfy the aspirations of billions of people.

Set aside any lingering questions about the data and about scientific uncertainty. Accept the worst-case scenarios of global warming, sea-level rising, and resulting problems. If, as Gore said, global warming is a moral issue, it is still necessary to compare the cost of the solutions with the benefits and to understand the costs and benefits of doing nothing.

Would it be more immoral to allow millions of people living on river deltas from Louisiana to Bangladesh to be flooded out or to hold back the industrial development of Asia and Africa and condemn billions of other people to lives of great poverty?

An environmentalist response to this is that Western economic prosperity is too expensive to extend to the rest of the world and is probably not sustainable even in the West over any long period of time. This may be true, but we should not accept it without a fight.

Sustaining Progress

The United Nations says sustainable development is a pattern of development suitable "to meet the needs of the present without compromising the ability of future generations to meet their own needs."

A good example is forest management: If you want lumber now and in the future, you shouldn't cut trees faster than they can grow back. But such sensible advice can lead advocates of sustainable development to oppose the consumption of finite resources. That can turn into a mandate to reduce the living standard of the world or the number of people in the world.

Working on this task are international and national councils on sustainable development. The U.S. council was created in 1993, with a mission to advise the president on issues of sustainable development. Its official mission statement declares

"Our vision is of a life-sustaining Earth. We are committed to achievement of a dignified, peaceful, and equitable existence. A sustainable United States will have a growing economy that provides equitable opportunities for satisfying livelihoods and a safe, healthy, high quality of life for current and future generations. Our nation will protect its environment, its natural resource base, and the functions and viability of natural systems on which all life depends."

The only thing missing is an indication of how this mission can be accomplished.

It's a good thing for us living today that there was no Council on Sustainable Development in 1830. The council would have seen that America was using up its wood faster than nature could replace the trees. Everybody knew that coal was too difficult to mine by hand and transport by horse and wagon, and nobody wanted the stuff, anyway, because it would not burn well in fireplaces. Nobody knew anything about petroleum, oil burners, or internal-combustion engines. Sustainable development would have required the preservation of our precious forest fuels, reduction of immigration, and careful husbanding of capital to avoid wasteful investment, especially in dangerous ideas like new fireplace grates and steam engines.

Sustainable development must not require frozen development, frozen technology, and frozen brains. Our descendants, whether they live in suburbs or space habitats, will be amused by our pitiful efforts to save some semblance of our way of life for them to enjoy. To them, their way of life will seem superior to ours—just as today ours seems superior to that of the hardscrabble farmers and homespun town folk of 1830. We should be thankful that our ancestors did not presume to impose their way of life on us.

Ecological Economics and Vice Versa

Ecologists have taught for a century and more that everything in the environment is connected to everything else. The Greek root "eco" means household. In ecology, the household is a metaphor for the planet Earth and for its subdivisions. The suffix "-logy" means "the study or knowledge of," as it does in all the science-naming words—biology, zoology, and so on. Ecologists study the relationships among animals, plants, and microorganisms—connected through the network of predation. Everything eats, and everything is also food for something else, directly or indirectly. The whole relationship creates the conditions in which the entire ecosystem survives beyond the lifespan of its parts.

Economists also find that everything is connected to everything else—through money. In economics, the "eco-" prefix denoting a household is a metaphor for human relationships using money, and the suffix "-nomics" refers to rules, customs, or laws.

The laws of economics are not legislated; they have been formulated from observation—like the way ecologists study biosystems. Consider one of the most important economic laws—the law of supply and demand—and how much it is like certain observations of ecologists.

Because value and wealth arise from scarcity, markets and market prices have evolved to measure the scarcity of things. Prices go up when goods are scarce; they go down when goods are abundant. This is the law of supply and demand, but it really should be known as the law of constantly changing prices: People's desires change constantly, and a market reflects their changing desires.

In an ecosystem, physical conditions constantly change, benefiting or harming members of the system. Take this oversimplified example: On the plains of Africa, dry conditions may reduce fodder for wildebeests, zebras, and other herbivores. If these animals are weakened, they may become easier prey, reducing the effort carnivores need to sustain themselves and reproduce. Dry weather thus foreshadows a larger population of predators. In the longer run, more predators will consume the excess food supply, which will leave the predators contending for scarce food and reduce their numbers.

Surpluses and deficits are the rule of nature, and so the law of supply and demand is a natural force. The markets humans use to respond to the surpluses and deficits of things with which they seek to sustain themselves are every bit as natural as humans themselves. Friedrich A. Hayek, a great free-market economist of the twentieth century, said that if the market were an invention suddenly brought into being next week, we should hail it as one of the greatest advances in human history. Unfortunately for the political cause of capitalism, markets have existed so long that many people despise them and regard prices set in markets as unnatural and unfair.

Where do market prices come from? Think of another natural process. Think of a cow path, a trail through the woods that leads from a pasture to a pond. Where did the trail come from? Cows tramped it down. Without the power of reason or the ability to communicate, cows agreed on the most desirable route from the pasture to the pond. When cows were first let into the pasture, we may imagine, each cow acted independently and took its own random path to the water. Accidentally, one larger cow, or a group of lucky cows, found a route that was slightly more advantageous. More cows herded together on that route and soon increased the advantage of that route by tramping down undergrowth, learning the places where a cow might stumble and protecting themselves from predators by sticking together in the herd.

People in a herd are more complex: They want more than a good pasture and a drink of water, but like cows, they find they can satisfy their needs and wants in a group.

A student of history might believe that the most common forms of human social organization are bonds imposed by force. From tribes following a strong chief to empires ancient and modern, history is a series of stories rarely relieved by voluntary cooperation. Everywhere in history books, armies collide and conquer. The individuals in the history stories are powerful leaders who forced thousands of anonymous, insignificant persons to accomplish feats worth writing about hundreds of years later. But the great deeds of great numbers of armed men were supported and fed by people who were making their way in life as best they could. Beneath the perception of the emperor, king, or duke were the villages and village markets, organized by necessity and happenstance, which made life a little easier by creating the opportunity for free exchanges enriching both parties.

The armies did not create wealth; they stole it. The specialization and division of labor made possible by markets created wealth.

Adam Smith and the Division of Labor

Some may say that Adam Smith, the eighteenth-century moral philosopher from Glasgow, should not be the central character in a discussion of environmental economics. But society is the human environment and Smith contributed greatly to understanding society. Combining morality and reality made him the first great economist. Smith emphasized the importance of the division of labor as the root of economic progress. He rejected the idea that national wealth was expressed in piles of gold and silver. He stressed above all that national and personal wealth are the result of industriousness and creativity, rather than luck or false dealing.

His enormous book, *An Inquiry into the Nature and Causes of the Wealth of Nations*, begins in philosophy and psychology with the question: What motivates people? Smith's answers include, importantly, "the desire of bettering our condition." People are rarely if ever satisfied with their condition, he observes, and to improve themselves, they naturally trade among themselves, seeking from others what they desire and offering to others what they have but do not esteem.

This is the important difference between the ecological study of natural systems and the economic study of humans and markets. People, capable of reason and prediction, can trade. The closest equivalent to trade that has evolved in nature is the symbiotic relationship, such as the tiny clown fish that eats by cleaning the sea anemone and is in turn protected by the anemone's tentacles. The difference is that animals don't choose their ecological relationships. People do choose their economic relationships: They choose what betters their conditions.

Smith tells us that trade completely founded on self-interest can improve the condition of both sides of a trade. Charity and kindness, although morally praiseworthy, are neither as powerful nor as useful as self-interested trade. In a famous passage, he declared: "It is not from the benevolence of the butcher, the brewer, or the baker that we expect our dinner, but from their regard to their own interest. We address ourselves not to their humanity but to their self-love, and never talk to them of our necessities but of their advantages. Nobody but a beggar chooses to depend chiefly upon the benevolence of their fellow-citizens."

As with animals in nature, society is a war of all against all, and at the same time an accidentally cooperative venture in mutual satisfaction. Smith said an individual laboring for himself "neither intends to promote the public interest, nor knows how much he is promoting it." Nor cares, nor should care, as Smith went on: "By directing his industry in such a manner as its produce may be of the greatest value, he intends only his own gain, and he is in this, as in many other cases, led by an invisible hand to promote an end which was no part of his intention. Nor is it always the worse for the society that it was not part of it. By pursuing his own interest he frequently promotes that of the society more effectually than when he really intends to promote it. I have never known much good done by those who affected to trade for the public good."

Adam Smith considered the division of labor to be the most important principle contributing to the wealth of people and nations. In a famous passage, he talked of the pin industry. When he wrote in the eighteenth century, metal pins were just becoming available to a mass market, and he told the reader how:

"In the way which this business is now carried on, not only is the whole work a peculiar trade, but it is divided into a number of branches, of which the greater part are also peculiar trades. One man draws out the wire, another straights it, a third cuts it, a fourth points it, a fifth grinds at the top for receiving the head; to make the head requires two or three distinct operations; to put it on is a peculiar business, to whiten the pins is another; it is even a trade by itself to put them into the paper.... I have seen a small manufactory of this kind where ten men only were employed, and where [each person averaged production of] 4,800 pins a day. But if they had all wrought separately and independently, and without any of them having been educated to this business, they certainly could not each of them make twenty, perhaps not one pin in a day."

The capitalist pin-factory owner invested his money, energy, insight, and leadership to make ten people vastly more productive together than the ten could be each on their own. It was this extra productivity—and the wages that the productivity could sustain—that drew millions of yeomen and subsistence farmers off the land and into the mills of Europe and America during the next 200 years.

Ecological Accounting

People focused on making a profit must attempt to increase revenues and reduce costs. Reducing costs, however, can take many forms; one common one is shifting a cost onto someone else without compensating them. The cost of generating electricity, for example, includes the cost of fuel, but it should include the cost of scrubbing exhaust gases to avoid harm to others who have no defense against breathing polluted air.

In the long run, our ecological books must balance. Inputs—energy from the sun and material from the dust of local space—eventually must equal outputs. Fossil fuels, for example, are the remnants of solar energy stored by plants hundreds of millions of years ago.

The long run is really long. Global warming and cooling is a process of trapping a little bit more or less solar energy under the atmospheric greenhouse of water vapor, carbon dioxide, and other gases. Over the last million years, the oceans have gone up and down by hundreds of feet dozens of times; glaciers have come and gone; deserts have been made and unmade. Over the last couple hundred million years, continents have been rearranged; mountains have risen higher than the Himalayas and eroded as flat as Kansas.

Species have come, changed, and gone. Climate changed in African jungles a few million years ago, offering a species of ape a chance to take its rudimentary use of tools onto broad plains. The apes prospered, grew smarter, and walked taller. Eventually we ape descendants spread over the entire earth and changed it.

Far more than 90 percent of species known to have existed on earth are extinct. We apes are not responsible for most of the disappearances. Dinosaurs vanished long before we apes tinkered with greenhouse-gas emissions; an asteroid, or a group of them, smashed into the earth and killed nearly everything. Some of the survivors evolved into birds. The dinosaurs vanished, indeed, but the eagle, chicken, and robin are their heirs.

Our technology is changing so quickly that we should not look beyond a century or so. What we cannot do today may well be cheap and easy in 2100.

Every Earth Day we hear calls for so-called sustainable development. This could mean little or no Western-style development for the people of underdeveloped countries because there won't be the resources or wealth to bring them to Western levels of development. It could condemn hundreds of millions of subsistence farmers to that grim life—and their children, and their children's children, unto the nth generation.

We apes have been around only a few million years, and we must take a shorter view. If we are going to survive, we must continue to design an environment that suits us. It is up to us to make development sustainable, not to choose only those lifestyles we imagine have naturally infinite possibilities. Nothing does.

It may not be worth investigating too seriously what the limits to growth really may be. If it's really inescapable that the carrying capacity of Earth for human existence is considerably smaller than today's population, and that the blessings of a polyester society cannot be extended for the foreseeable future to so many billions of people as are now living, then what?

Eat, drink, and be merry, for tomorrow the human race dies? Whether in a plague, a famine, or a Maoist fit of population control, if our passing is inevitable, the manner of our passing would hardly matter, any more than the exact size of the fatal asteroid mattered to the dinosaurs.

The real limits to growth are the limits of our technology and the limits imposed by our politics. Our investments in energy research and development should be aimed at the creation of new technologies and economic opportunities that people can use to improve their lives. In a primitive place, that could be commissioning the design of a more fuel-efficient wood stove, but only until it's possible to install electric transmission lines that don't waste so much power and thus bring the benefits of electricity to more customers at a lower cost.

Here we have to account for profit as well as policy. An honest government investing tax money might commission the stove design, the power lines, or both, based on politicians' calculation of what will please the citizens. As likely, a crooked government will direct investment capital to officials' foreign bank accounts, while blaming outside forces for the failure to show results.

Profit, however, is a sterner master. Capital must go where risk-adjusted returns are greatest.

Tragedies of the Commons

At some times and some places, risk-adjusted returns on investment are illusory. Environmental economists frequently talk of "externalities," by which they mean costs, such as pollution, that are dumped on the world at large without charge to the person or business doing the dumping. A railroad built across a pasture becomes a danger to the grazing cattle. Farmers may have tried to get the railroad to fence in their right-of-way; this did not always work. In the pre-industrial age, laws dealing with this issue were weak. Always and everywhere laws are weak when lawmakers attempt to impose costs on strong economic institutions. The long struggle to impose environmental regulations on polluters is well known.

Not as well known is another form of collision between private rights and public interests. Those who invest in the harvesting of wild resources may have a private right to do so, but the public interest may lie in limiting that harvest so that it does not go beyond the maximum sustainable yield. Problems arise with particular force when the maximum sustainable yield is not known.

In recent decades, it has begun to look as if overfishing is the natural result of the pursuit of fish. Salmon of the Oregon coast, cod of the Grand Banks, haddock of New England waters, and even lowly pollock, herring, and capelin of the open Atlantic and Pacific oceans are going the way of oysters, rockfish, bluefish, and so many other overfished near-shore species.

The overdevelopment of the North Atlantic fisheries was accomplished with factory trawler ships. The first of these vessels was launched in 1954, a triumph of new technology using nylon nets, net-retrieval ramps, skinning and filleting machines, and freezing machines. The big ship could travel from Europe to the Grand Banks off Newfoundland, fish for a longer period of time, and bring home frozen fish ready for market, of higher value than salt fish or iced fish of dubious freshness.

By 1974, hundreds of such ships existed. They ranged farther into the world's oceans because the North Atlantic catch had already peaked in 1968. A couple years later, the maritime nations of the world agreed to establish 200-mile exclusion zones out from their coasts, in which only their own fishermen, and any foreigners they might license, could fish.

Facing no competition, fishermen of many countries, including the U.S. and Canada, invested heavily in new boats and equipment. Soon they were overfishing their waters even more thoroughly than foreigners had.

All this is an economic problem called the "tragedy of the commons," referring to the village fields of the English feudal system. Each villager had an equal right to graze sheep and cows on the village's common property. Result: Overgrazing. In a 1968 *Science Magazine* article of that name, Garrett Hardin laid the foundation for an important field in environmental economics.

He summed up the incentives: "Each man is locked into a system that compels him to increase his herd without limit—in a world that is limited. Ruin is the destination toward which all men rush, each pursuing his own best interest in a society that believes in the freedom of the commons. Freedom in a commons brings ruin to all."

Compare the fishing vessels to cattle on a common pasture. Compare the fish to blades of grass. The owners of vessels rushed to build new efficient ships to capture the free wealth that swims in the ocean, as the owners of cattle had to increase their herds to capture the free nutrients locked in each blade of grass.

The ecologically economic problem of the commons lies in the private ownership of the means of production and the common ownership—no ownership at all—of the raw material. Ranchers are subject to the same incentive on the range; miners encounter it in a gold rush.

Hardin has asked some of the really hard questions posed by the tragedy of the commons: Would Americans have more or less to eat if we had not commonized the risk of farming through government subsidies? Would our residences be more secure against floods, not built on flood plains, if we had not commonized disaster relief? Will the people in very poor countries ever limit their numbers if rich countries commonize their survival through food aid?

So much sustainability depends on the organization of property. An unmanaged commons invites disaster. A managed commons begs the question of how to select a manager and how to control the manager's power .

The practical solution to the conflict between private interest and public interest is more private interest. Private enclosure of the commons yields private benefits, private costs, and a profit-and-loss statement.

Many modern people have only a dim idea of the Industrial Revolution, filtered through poet William Blake's line about "dark, Satanic mills," and filtered through the misery and poverty portrayed in Charles Dickens's novels. The story they know is that enclosure of the common pasture drove innocent peasants off the fields and into the mills, that the people of England suffered greatly from the destruction of the old rural way of life and suffered again from the oppression of urban factory bosses. The story implies that rural folk would have been better off if there had never been an Industrial Revolution. Some imagine child labor in factories to have been a greater evil than child labor in the fields. Some imagine poverty in the city to be more unnatural than poverty as a tenant farmer.

Some historians now see that enclosure promoted growth. The conversion of common pasture to wheat fields was one of many ways of increasing yield per acre, which in turn increased rents, which in turn made capitalists out of landlords, which in turn made factory investment possible, which in turn created new wealth and new jobs. Prosperity spread so widely that England's population nearly doubled from 10.5 million in 1801 to 18.1 million in 1840. More efficient private farming fed the multitude. The tragedy of the English commons became the triumph of the English economy.

We must not imagine that the carrying capacity of the English soil, or the Earth, is like the carrying capacity of a wagon, not only finite but unchangeable. In reality, the Conestoga wagon becomes a Boeing 747, with a different range, speed, and carrying capacity.

Technology and property rights can solve the tragedy of the commons. Even on the ocean, the unlimited right to fish can be turned into the property right to farm. Creation of exclusive economic zones was a good first step and must be taken further. Each country that wants to fish should sell fishing rights. The higher that scarcity drives the price of fish and fish meal, the more that fishermen will bid for the right to catch fish. The funds raised can be used to establish saltwater hatcheries and to develop the technology of mariculture. While international corporations would probably do the job best, even American state governments manage to turn a profit on trout streams and fishing licenses.

The true tragedy of the commons was that feudalism offered no incentive to improve the land. It demanded impossible cooperation from people who could have prospered in competitive freedom.

A Flood of Problems

An environmental policy ordered by profit would tackle current problems. To mention a problem of recent note in the United States, we should change land-use rules to foster development of new towns in areas safe from floods. Paying for new levees and rebuilding parts of New Orleans that are below sea level just engraves an invitation for new environmental disaster.

Against all reason, the federal government has issued new flood regulations that will let people in New Orleans rebuild homes that should never have been built in the first place and reinsure rebuilt homes through renewed federal flood insurance that should never have been issued in the first place.

Some homes that flooded up to their attics are considered eligible for flood insurance if the home sites are raised three feet. Even that inadequate defense will not be required unless the Katrina flood substantially damaged more than half the house. Some two-story homes won't have to be raised at all.

Amazingly short-sighted city residents and officials greeted the new maps as important good news for New Orleans because so much more of the city can be rebuilt than would have been the case if the maps of flood-prone areas had been more realistic.

Rebuilding New Orleans this way means putting citizens in the middle of another disaster, and it means the next disaster will also be subsidized by the rest of the country. It's a losing proposition, throwing good money after bad.

The same irresponsible process that built New Orleans and rebuilt it several times is at work in other places. In northern California, a danger point is the city of Sacramento and the river delta between the state capital and the San Francisco Bay. At least 400,000 people live or work in the shadow of levees that engineers say are much less secure than those that protected New Orleans. And the cities of northern California are closing in on each other, with new suburbs proposed for sites as much as 20 feet below water level.

Stopping irresponsible development, or at least refusing to subsidize the insurance that makes it possible, is the most important kind of flood-prevention investment. The distant flood prevention offered by the struggle against global warming is sheer speculation by comparison with the sound investment of preventing foolish development. There is no certainty of a payoff from reducing carbon-dioxide emissions—the planet was warming for 10,000 years before there were any industrial emissions. If industrial emissions were eliminated, the planet might keep warming. Floods, however, follow the law of gravity—they never inundate the high ground. It's a lot cheaper to move people to high ground before the next flood.

Summary

The economy is an ecology, and vice versa. We cannot expect to solve environmental challenges without investing wisely.

3

A Capitalist Prescription for Trade: Free Exchange Enriches Both Sides of Every Deal

Free trade is the power to ignore borders and boundaries on the road to wealth and progress.

For a demonstration of the benefits of free trade, look to the world's largest, oldest, and most prosperous free-trade zone, the United States of America. If the United States were 50 countries with 50 currencies and 50 protectionist legislatures, it would look like Old Europe or Latin America. Even if these 50 countries were fortunate enough to avoid wars over trade, they would never be as rich in material goods or opportunity as the United States is today. Each state might be prosperous within the limits of its natural advantages, but as a single country with a constitutional prohibition on interstate barriers to trade, each of the United States draws on the bounty and skills of all the others.

New York can import produce from New Jersey, milk from Pennsylvania, skilled workers from Connecticut, electricity from Massachusetts, natural gas from Louisiana, clothing from North Carolina, manufactured goods from Ohio, and vegetables from California. And if any of these states fails to satisfy New Yorkers, they can turn to the products and people of other states.

In turn, New York can sell everything it makes and all its services to these and all the other states. There are regulations and taxes imposed by each state, but no state can impose tariffs, quotas, or exclusive marketing rights without running afoul of the U.S. Constitution. The Constitution, indeed, says a great deal more about free domestic trade than it does about seemingly more important rights, such as free speech or the protection of private property. Prohibitions in Article I, Sections 8 and 9, include:

- "No tax or duty shall be laid on articles exported from any state."

- "No preference shall be given by any regulation of commerce or revenue to the ports of one state over those of another, nor shall vessels bound to, or from, one state be obliged to enter clear or pay duties in another...."

- "No state shall, without the consent of Congress, lay any imposts or duties on imports or exports, except what may be absolutely necessary for executing its inspection laws, and the net produce of all duties and imposts shall be for the use of the Treasury of the United States...."

- "The Congress shall have power...to regulate commerce with foreign nations and among the several states...."

- "All duties, imposts and excises, shall be uniform throughout the United States."

The delegates to the Constitutional Convention had just been through a war that they started in part to win freedom of trade; they were determined to avoid the conflicts that take place when business crosses national borders.

Founding Traders

The first successful English colony in North America, Jamestown in Virginia, was settled in 1607 by a private corporation seeking private wealth. For more than a century afterward, British policy neglected the American colonies. It wasn't practical to do much more than send a governor and a few soldiers—the Americans had to fend for themselves economically and govern themselves politically. After 150 years of such benign neglect, the American colonials considered benign neglect their natural right. But as Britain's maritime power grew, it sought to control more commerce with the colonies. A series of Navigation Acts sought to keep foreign ships out of American ports and prevent American ships from trading with foreign countries. The goal was to enrich British shipping and British traders at the expense of higher costs for the colonials.

Among the many abuses of British colonial power listed in the Declaration of Independence, trade restrictions loom large. But victory for the new nation did not settle the issues of trade that helped create it. Where the British had set trade policy to enrich its businesses, some Americans sought to follow.

Alexander Hamilton, who was Secretary of the Treasury for President George Washington, issued a "Report on Manufactures" to the Congress, in which he recommended that Congress make the United States economically independent of Europe. In Hamilton's view, the United States could not compete with more advanced countries, particularly England, in manufacturing. He thought a free-trade policy would render the U.S. a permanently agrarian society, supplying grain and taking goods. He asserted that the reason for America's inability to compete was European manufacturing subsidies and concluded that the new country would have to do the same to advance and prosper. He recommended protective tariffs, the creation of a national bank modeled on the Bank of England, subsidies for manufacturing, and limits on trade—policies more than somewhat reminiscent of the British restrictions on the colonies that had touched off the Revolutionary War.

Hamilton carried the day on the tariff—it became the federal government's primary source of revenue—but lost on the question of direct industrial subsidies. He did encourage creating corporations to build industries and backed the Society for Useful Manufactures, a freewheeling corporation in New Jersey that planned and eventually built the nation's first industrial park where the falls of the Passaic River offered convenient water power.

Vicious political battles over the questions of finance and economics lasted through the Federalist Washington and Adams administrations and into the Democratic-Republican administration of Thomas Jefferson. The Federalists fell into factions that had little to do with economics, and one of the factional disputes saw Aaron Burr and Hamilton so much at loggerheads that they fought a duel in 1804, in which Hamilton was killed.

The Constitution effectively provided a free-trade area within the country, but with a high tariff wall to shelter it. That national tariff was more effective than state tariffs because no state could raise its tariff very high without prompting competition from neighboring states.

In the 1820s, the tariff issue began to divide the country along the lines of North and South, just as slavery was dividing it. The North's interest favored a high tariff to protect New England's manufacturing from competition, especially British competition. The South's interest was selling cotton to English and French mills and using the profits to buy manufactured goods at the lowest possible price. In turn, Europeans who could not sell as much to America could not buy as much from America.

Senator Daniel Webster of New Hampshire was not a man of narrow political loyalty. He fought the tariff that many New Englanders favored because he understood opportunity cost: "The true inquiry is, can we produce the article at the same cost, or nearly the same cost at which we can import it?" He saw that if Americans could not, they should import it and find something more useful to do with their capital and labor.

Under the U.S. Constitution, a burning national issue is almost never really settled. With elections to the House of Representatives and one-third of the Senate every two years, and presidential elections every four years, anything the people's representatives do can be reversed. Slavery was settled, but only with extra-Constitutional means, at the high cost of a civil war. Tariffs and other forms of protectionism, taxation, federalism, and all the economic issues of the Washington administration remain with us today.

Restraint of Trade

The important issue in international trade is the power of governments to interfere with it. Everything else can be settled in the marketplace. Governments, attempting to please a small percentage of their citizens by protecting them from foreign competition, push their populations toward poverty. A country that protects farmers does so at the expense of all who eat. A country that protects auto workers does so at the expense of all who drive. Free trade, on the other hand, enlarges markets and creates prosperity everywhere it is tried. It also forces change on the companies and individuals who face competition with foreign goods and services that are cheaper or better than theirs. This is highly desirable in general, but painful in particular.

A small dispute between two neighbors illustrates the difficulty. Canadian two-by-four lumber holds up about one-third of houses constructed in the U.S. The American timber industry doesn't like this, and it complained for years that Canadian provincial governments, especially British Columbia's, didn't charge Canadian woodcutters as much to cut on public lands as Americans are charged by their state and federal governments. The only appropriate Canadian answer to this was, "So? What business is that of Americans?" But the American answer was to charge 20 percent tariffs on Canadian lumber to make up for the allegedly unfair discounting.

An international panel set up to decide trade disputes ruled in favor of the Canadians over and over again. But the American government's position was that Canada should negotiate—apparently on the principle that "what's mine is mine and what's yours is negotiable."

Eventually the two countries negotiated, and the only losers were consumers. The U.S. paid back $4 billion of the $5 billion it had collected from Canadian lumber exporters, and the Canadian industry agreed not to increase its exports. To enforce that "voluntary" restriction, the Canadian government agreed to collect a tax on lumber exports if the price of lumber in the U.S. fell below a certain price.

Americans should have been delighted if Canadians wanted to subsidize their forest-product industries and make Americans pay less for home building. We also shouldn't mind when Canadians sell us oil and natural gas from Alberta, electricity from Ontario and Quebec, or Broadway-bound theatrical productions created in Toronto, all of which are subsidized one way or another by the Canadian government. It's in America's short-term, selfish interest not to do anything to make them reconsider their generous policies in any sector they subsidize.

Having real free trade in lumber might even have focused American forest-product companies on the American lawmakers and regulators who compromised their efficiency and blighted their operations with ill-conceived regulatory policies. The more important beneficiaries, as always, would be American consumers. The housing boom in the U.S. that started in 2003 made the U.S.-Canadian lumber dispute less relevant. Demand for lumber was so strong that it pushed prices up enough to satisfy U.S. producers, and it also enriched Canadian producers. Lumber mills on both sides of the border expanded capacity. Unfortunately for all of them, the boom didn't last. By the end of 2007, house-building was in a definite recession. Even the newest and most efficient lumber mills were retrenching, laying off workers and cutting production. The stage was set for producers and consumers to renew their trade dispute.

The Productive Power of Outsourcing

The most important power of free trade is the opportunity for competition and choice. Consumers choose between domestic and foreign cars or among shoes imported from many different countries with different qualities, styles, and prices. They are better off for having the freedom to choose. Even if they patronize domestic producers, they usually enjoy lower prices or higher quality than they might if the local goods faced no foreign competition.

For every such decision consumers make, business executives in the commercial web make thousands. Nearly every component of their business, from nuts and bolts to accounting services, can be done in-house or by outside suppliers, even if they are located overseas.

Business executives must compare every facet of their production cost in the U.S. with their production cost in another place. Centralizing any business has advantages, but cheaper materials might be obtained abroad and imported. Or cheaper labor might be the crucially attractive factor of production.

The United States has been outsourcing its least-productive jobs to Mexico and Asia for decades. It is one of the least-recognized sources of the productivity boom that began in the 1980s. (Other sources include lower taxes and advancing technological leverage.) When the "giant sucking sound" that Ross Perot warned about in the 1994 debate over the North American Free Trade Agreement (NAFTA) sucks away a textile worker's factory job in North Carolina, it creates two or three jobs in Haiti or China because labor is cheaper there and factories are much less mechanized. If the U.S. worker gets another low-paying manufacturing job, productivity probably goes up because only the jobs that produce goods with more value added remain in the U.S. Even if the textile worker goes on unemployment, total U.S. productivity might be enhanced because using a worker to produce cheap goods drags down productivity. Taking the worker out of the productivity calculation entirely is statistically better. There is an even better answer for the laid-off workers and the economy: former workers should go to school or get job training to add to their human capital. The real goal should be to qualify them for higher-paying, more productive jobs in other industries.

Globalization clarifies why some countries are poor. Beyond the ravages of war, disease, and corruption, some countries are poor because they would rather be poor and proud than get richer following the examples of rich countries.

That's frequently on display at World Trade Organization (WTO) meetings, when trade ministers from poor countries walk out of negotiations that could make their countries richer, and rich countries persevere in policies that harm their own citizens.

Trade negotiations, like trade wars, are best seen as wars between governments and their own people.

"If the developed countries had offered more to the developing countries, it would have created an atmosphere more conducive to a settlement," said a delegate from Jamaica, explaining to a *Washington Post* reporter why developing countries walked out of WTO negotiations at Cancun, Mexico, in 2003.

The U.S. and Europe said they were prepared to reduce agricultural export subsidies in return for poorer countries' putting lower tariffs on industrial goods. But a group of 21 relatively poor countries, including Brazil, China, India, Indonesia, and South Africa, did not want to make a deal. They preferred to denounce the United States and the European Union for trying to dictate to them. They were more intent on preserving their own forms of protectionism, which benefit their own special interests, than they were in tearing down the production and export subsidies that industrial countries lavish on their farmers.

The Cancun meeting was part of the Doha Round of trade negotiations, begun by the WTO in Doha, Qatar, in 2001. All parties had agreed at Doha the goal was to reduce agricultural trade barriers. The question turned out to be, "Whose trade barriers?" and the answer was "not mine."

As is so often the case in trade negotiations, each side would have been better off if it had taken the other side's advice. Industrial nations do not make themselves richer by catering to their farmers. Their agricultural future probably requires adoption of industrial farming of commodities on one hand and gourmet truck gardening on small patches of land on the other. These are both enterprises that can stand on their own. Subsidies keep too much land too intensively cultivated and produce gargantuan surpluses that have to be disposed of at a loss. If industrial countries took the advice of poor countries, they could have cheaper commodities and lower government spending.

The poor countries can't make their citizens better off through trade restrictions that raise prices and reduce supplies of everything they import. If they took the advice of industrial countries, they could have more capital investment in agriculture and industry, more productive jobs, and higher wages.

Countries such as India, Bangladesh, Pakistan, Guatemala, Vietnam, and most of those in Africa have economies heavily dependent on agriculture for the little bit of wealth they can create. Agriculture's share of gross domestic product (GDP) ranges up to 45 percent in Tanzania. Not coincidentally, most of its poor people live in rural areas.

William R. Cline, an economist at the Center for Global Development, calculates that eliminating U.S. and European agricultural export subsidies and import restrictions would reduce their overproduction of agricultural commodities. That would increase food prices on world markets, which might not seem like a good thing for poor countries, but it would increase income in the rural areas of poor countries more than it would increase expenses for their urban poor, he says. Cline estimates that about 200 million of the world's poorest people would receive significant boosts in income if the world could agree on unsubsidized free trade in agriculture.

The shoe also fits the other foot. By Cline's estimate, if poor countries abandoned their self-defeating trade restrictions and opened themselves more completely to trade and investment, 450 million of the world's poor—many of them farmers—could find more productive work and lift themselves up.

Industrialization in a more open economy rapidly increases opportunity and hope. If Mexico, for example, earns only 4 percent of its GDP from agriculture and 32 percent of its poor people are still scratching out a marginal existence on the land, then most of those farmers need a more productive way of making a living..

Economics is not always a dismal science. Sometimes it points the way to wealth creation and eventual prosperity for those willing to see it.

The Doha Round collapsed a couple times in a general demand for more concessions from the other side. But the deal that's been on the table for discussion can be accepted by either side. Free trade can be unilateral because it enriches countries that practice it, even if their trading partners aren't so wise. The citizens of free-trading countries are guaranteed the lowest possible prices for everything they consume, whereas their counterparts in protectionist countries face artificial scarcities and high prices. Producers in free-trading countries are pushed to compete in their home markets by cutting costs to the absolute minimum, and if they are exporters, they face high hurdles in hostile countries, which they can only overcome with world-class salesmanship and low costs. If they try hard enough and succeed, they become more productive and wealthier.

Consider Hong Kong. The former British Crown colony has no natural economic advantages. It is not much more than a large rock with millions of people clinging to it, yet it prospers, even under Communist control, because it has free trade. And Hong Kong does free trade the brilliantly easy way: It declared free trade unilaterally. No negotiations, no trade-offs, no exchanges of political favors.

The squabbling nations of the WTO should have as much courage as Hong Kong. Even the wealthiest would gain, but the poorest would gain the most.

The world's diplomats and politicians consider these issues to be more complicated. Most countries protect some industries, and a few countries protect practically every economic activity. They make their economic choices based on domestic politics and their politicians' biased estimates of their national interests.

In the U.S., the government caves in to timber interests, to steel, and to other industries that have stagnated under the smothering embrace of protectionism. It's not even cost-effective. Other Americans have to pay for the expense of protecting jobs from foreign competitors or from outsourcing, and the cost often far exceeds the value of the jobs saved in the U.S. economy. Steel jobs, for example, pay less than $50,000 a year, but a system of quotas and tariffs protected jobs in steel for years at a cost of $800,000 per job. That's like giving away $10 bills to steelworkers and getting back 68 cents as a thank you.

The U.S. government also protects farmers from competition with low-cost imported crops. Sugar, grain, and citrus are among the most important products Latin American countries would immediately be able to export in greater quantities if the U.S. opened all its agricultural markets to trade competition. The protected U.S. farmers who consider them important could grow other crops.

Make Jobs—Don't Protect Them

If you had been hanging around Greenville, Michigan, in spring 2004, you might have seen a bus full of union activists pull up and deliver a ready-made demonstration. Their signs demanded, "Show Us the Jobs." The 51 out-of-work bus riders hailed from every state, plus the District of Columbia, and the union folks who hired the bus and organized the passengers hoped to impress upon the nation that Bush administration policies and attitudes were to blame for the loss of millions of jobs to other countries.

When they arrived in Greenville, at the site of a refrigerator factory owned by the Swedish appliance company Electrolux, the protestors denounced a company plan to close the plant and terminate 2,700 workers while sinking $195 million over the next few years into the construction of a new plant in Juarez, Mexico, that would employ 3,000 Mexicans. Wages in Mexico would start at roughly one-tenth the wages Electrolux paid in Michigan.

"Giant sucking sound," anyone? What could be a clearer example of the kind of outsourcing that sacrifices American jobs on the altar of free trade? That's what the bus riders said, anyway. They made a lot of noise in that vein, though they apparently were deaf to the thundering irony that Electrolux is a Swedish company. The American jobs being outsourced were Swedish jobs that were outsourced to America years earlier.

Electrolux is an international company, based in Sweden but manufacturing in more than 50 countries and selling appliances in nearly every country in the world. It is a survivor in a difficult industry. Electrolux didn't become the biggest appliance company in the world by staying in one place. In the same season of 2004, the company also announced a plant closing in Durham, England, and plans to build new factories in Thailand and India. It was getting ready to shut a vacuum-cleaner factory in Sweden and replace it with production from a factory in Hungary.

Without constantly calculating cost-effectiveness, companies don't survive and don't employ anybody. Focusing on the 2,700 workers in Greenville caused the riders to miss several points.

Other American jobs were also at stake, those to be preserved or created by the decision of Electrolux to move to Mexico. Employees of Electrolux appliance dealerships would have new products to sell at more attractive prices. Truckers would haul parts and material from the U.S. to Juarez during construction of the new factory and later haul refrigerators from Juarez to everywhere. U.S. businesses would equip and supply the new factory.

Other products, possibly of higher value and greater economic importance than refrigerators, might be made in the U.S. after the last refrigerator plant was gone. They could even be made in Greenville and by refugees from Greenville who moved to places with more opportunities—some of whom probably would be paid more than they ever would have earned at the Electrolux plant in Greenville.

On the whole, Americans have gained much more from open markets and the free movement of capital than they have lost. Specific losses like those in Greenville are painful and easy to blame on others, whereas profits, like those earned when a Japanese car company moved to Michigan, are too easily accepted as the just desserts paid to superior ability.

Complaining about outsourcing makes a political mountain out of an economic molehill. Critics of outsourcing cannot claim that as many as 1 million American jobs are exported in a year. Normal forces of job creation and job destruction in the U.S. economy eliminate at least 27 million jobs a year in good times. Because the American tradition of economic liberty is allowed to work, the U.S. economy creates more than 30 million jobs a year, even when growth is not particularly robust. (The Bureau of Labor Statistics tracks the ebb and flow of jobs in its quarterly report on Business Employment Dynamics, available on the BLS web site, www.bls.gov.) If unemployment grows in the next few years, the most likely cause will be demographic pressure, not trade; a new generation is arriving on the job market in greater numbers than the cohorts of the past 20 years.

The Benefits of Free Trade

Too many Americans see free trade as a painful form of foreign aid, in which we generous Yankees agree to take foreign goods and throw our own people out of work. They ignore the benefits of free trade, which are generated in four ways:

- **Expanded creativity and efficiency**—This is what the nineteenth-century English economist David Ricardo called comparative advantage. It is fairly obvious every country serves itself best by specializing in products it creates most efficiently and importing others made more cheaply elsewhere. The insight from Ricardo is that every country should specialize in what it does best even if it does not have an absolute advantage in any possible product.

- **Economies of scale**—Countries that specialize get better at their specialties because they concentrate on developing relevant skills among their workers and because they can spread fixed capital costs—such as machinery, communications, education, and research—over more units of output.

- **Technological spillover**—New technologies and strategies are distributed and adopted more quickly when many competitors seek an edge in a hotly contested market, even if some of the competitors are foreign.

- **Import competition**—Cheap imports force unprotected domestic producers to get better or collapse, even if they already thought they were world-class. Like whipping the horse leading the race, it may not be fair, but it often works.

Measuring these benefits is not simple. If it were, senators and presidents would do it, and the politics of trade wouldn't need to rely on scare tactics.

Economists Gary Hufbauer, Scott Bradford, and Paul Grieco ran gigabytes of data from many countries through econometric models created by the Organisation for Economic Co-operation and Development and other independent economic experts. The models ran with different assumptions and rules. Some put emphasis on macroeconomic policies and the growth of GDP per capita; others focused on microeconomic analysis of the behavior of firms. Another tried to analyze today's world as if the high tariffs of the 1930s had never been repealed by the many postwar rounds of trade negotiations, as if the U.S. had suddenly gone back to the Smoot-Hawley Tariff Act of 1930 and the rest of the world's nations retaliated as they did then.

No matter how they sliced and diced the numbers, they found that Americans benefit substantially from the past pains of trade liberalization. Between 7 percent and 13 percent of U.S. GDP has come to us each year as a result of loosened trade restrictions. That's net, after the costs to individuals who lost their jobs and the costs to firms that had to shut down. It's at least $980 billion a year, $3,200 per person, $8,500 per household. On the high end of the results, it could be $1.8 trillion a year for America—$6,000 for every person, $16,000 per household.

If objectors knew what they were saying when they denounced globalism and demanded level playing fields and international traffic cops, they would change their tunes. Wouldn't they? Perhaps not. Some Americans remember a land that never was, where all vegetables were locally grown, all stores were run by moms and pops who gave credit, all bankers were kindly benefactors of their communities, all unions won their rights in open bargaining and all politicians were honest.

Every year we get richer because we have reduced international trade barriers. We should keep reaching higher. If we go forward realistically, continuing to liberalize trade restrictions by lowering our barriers in agriculture, textiles, transport, and services, the three economists tell us we have more benefits to earn: As much as 12 percent more GDP annually could be produced with a complete free-trade regime that forces us to redeploy capital and labor to the sectors with the highest returns on investment.

Solving Our China Problem with Trade

Industrial capitalism requires mass markets. Mass markets require consumer sovereignty. A consumer allowed to choose among six brands of toothpaste eventually finds freedom of choice natural, and then it becomes natural to spit out tyrants in a new revolution, perhaps even to ignore them on such a grand scale that a violent revolution becomes unnecessary.

This is the point of the American policy toward China, just as it was the point of American policy toward the Soviet Union. Call it what you will—military containment, constructive engagement, peaceful coexistence—America rests its strategy on the economic strength of freedom. Facing political patience, military determination to deter conquest, and open-handed business deals of mutual advantage, socialism crumbles.

The Soviet Union opened its old autocratic economy out of sheer necessity. The path of slow starvation, as chosen by North Korea, was its only other option. China has also opened its old autocratic economy out of sheer necessity. Mass starvation has been replaced by rural development and urban economic growth. But even as they transform the economy, the old revolutionaries still profess that they are indispensable to maintaining order in a country that has often fallen into anarchy.

If we are determined and patient, trade will bring China the profits and wealth needed to make it stable enough to enjoy a weak government. While we trade with China to help its people, we should do the same for other countries. The denial of favorable status does nothing to bring a government to Somalia, liberalize the nations of former Indo-China and former Yugoslavia, feed the people of North Korea, or protect Sudanese refugees from the slaughter of Darfur. Trade sanctions are doing nothing to liberalize the Iranian theocracy or shake the thrones of dictators in Myanmar or Syria.

The most conspicuous failure of using trade for political ends is the U.S. trade embargo with Cuba. For nearly 50 years, Fidel Castro and his minions have been comfortable in power, blaming the U.S. embargo for all their economic mismanagement. Politically connected Cubans easily obtain from other countries anything their government permits them to have, whereas the government easily blames the U.S. embargo for its economic and social tyranny.

Trade Enriched without Conquest

In early times, only one relatively easy way existed to improve the productivity of land, labor, and capital: Moving products from a place where they were abundant to a place where they were scarce. Trading, across seas or deserts, added a new dimension beyond local supply and demand.

The owners of certain capital equipment, such as ships and camels, could move goods from a place of local surplus to a place where goods were greatly desired. Early traders risked their capital to purchase goods outright in hopes of selling them somewhere else, where they were more valued.

By trade, it was possible to become rich without conquest.

Some economists do not understand trade except as an enforcement of some kind of power. They assert that profit occurs because the trade parties operate from unequal strength, such as unequal possession of information, political subjugation, or a monopoly of buying or selling power.

If silk was common in China and scarce in Europe, as it was in the Middle Ages, a merchant who bought silk cheap in China and sold it dear in Europe served both places in addition to himself. He provided transportation and bore the risk of loss along the way, for which he was compensated as a service-provider and middle-man. But beyond that, he relieved China of something it had in excess and provided China with something it wanted—probably gold—while providing Europeans with something they wanted more than a particular quantity of gold. The merchant, the middle-man, relieved economic stress in both places.

Immobile merchants sitting in a bazaar, buying quickly and selling quickly, also perform a service that relieves economic stress. If three farmers sell baskets of apples, berries, and peaches to one fruit merchant, who then sells individual pieces of fruit to customers, the merchant has relieved the farmers of their excessive dependence on large quantities of their specific crops, saved them the trouble of finding buyers, and, of course, saved the individual customers the trouble of finding sellers.

The War God Demands Gold

In the history of wealth, the seventeenth century stands as the high point of a belief in state power and conquest. This belief drove all European countries, none more than France. Building on the comment of Machiavelli that for the state to be rich, the people must be poor, French mercantilist philosophers concluded that merchants must flourish so they could be taxed; then soldiers could be paid and the state could wage wars of conquest and defense.

"We must have money," said the philosopher Montchretien, "and if we have none from our own productions, then we must have some from foreigners." He advised his readers to purchase only what was essential from abroad, to tax imports, and to create manufacturing enterprises in France. All this was to make the nation more than self-sufficient so that it could earn more gold and silver by exporting. Above all, mercantilists recommended that their countries hoard their gold and silver.

The impossibility of conducting trade by enriching one's own country while beggaring all neighbors was lost on the mercantilists, who saw trade as war by other means. Victory in this kind of war, however, is defeat for the interests of the victorious country. A country with vast quantities of silver and gold cheapens the value of that bullion at home and drives up the prices of goods and services produced at home. It finds that imported goods are cheaper, except that it then subjects those goods to high tariffs and other restrictions: In other words, it drives its citizens to smuggling and black marketeering.

Montchretien's advice was taken up by French ministers, especially the Cardinals Richelieu and Mazarin, and later the Finance Minister Jean Baptiste Colbert. They added the idea of importing skilled workers from other countries and investing royal funds to establish the most advanced cloth, glass, and other industries in Europe. French workers were prohibited from emigrating. They also chartered monopolistic companies for trade with other lands and with colonies.

All the profits from such investments and from increasingly oppressive taxation vanished into the maw of war. In the first half of the seventeenth century, France was surrounded by hostile Hapsburgs in Austria and Spain. Richelieu and Mazarin played double and triple games of diplomacy during the Thirty Years War, sometimes allying France to Protestants in an effort to exhaust Spanish power.

It's impossible to tell if French mercantilism worked as an economic system. Perhaps it did, but only at the price of slower growth, monopolistic business practices, high prices, and low wages for workers. Colbert did leave behind one fine epigram that sums up his attitude to commerce: "The art of taxation consists in so plucking the goose as to obtain the largest amount of feathers with the least possible amount of hissing." It is certain that French national wealth was not enhanced by the mercantile combination of subsidized production at home, protectionist tariffs, foreign adventures, and absolute monarchical rule.

The mercantile system in every country tended to increase the probability of war, and with war, the centralization of government, because the mercantile system worked only with absolute power behind it. Mercantilists wondered where the money went and passed laws to keep it in their countries. They could not see that their laws actually promoted exporting capital to places where it could find higher returns.

The Earnings of Trade

David Hume of Edinburgh, Scotland, was among the first philosophers to reject mercantilism and the accumulation of gold and silver as the ends of statecraft. He noted how the surplus of precious metal simply drove up prices. In a 1752 essay, *Of Commerce*, he recommended that governments support foreign trade in both directions:

"By its imports [it] furnishes material for new manufactures and by its exports, it produces labour in particular commodities, which could not be consumed at home. In short, a kingdom that has a large import and export, must abound more with industry, and that employed upon delicacies and luxuries, than a kingdom which rests contended with its native commodities. It is, therefore, more powerful, as well as richer and happier."

David Ricardo's role as a politician was to argue for free trade at a time when England was protectionist. The Corn Laws set high prices for imported grain of all kinds; the government defended this as a matter of national security to a nation just finished with a quarter century of war. Ricardo built on Adam Smith's advice that every country and every region should specialize in what it can do better than anyone else. Smith's Principle of Absolute Advantage showed that, for example, England should raise sheep, make woolens, and import wine; France should raise grapes, make wine, and import woolens.

Fine as far as it went, but what if a nation is not better at anything? Or what if a nation is better at so many things that it cannot fully use its abilities for all of them? Ricardo took Smith's Principle of Absolute Advantage and created his Principle of Comparative

Advantage: Potential competitors should specialize in whatever they are best at, relative to all other things they might be able to do. They should follow the lures of maximum profit and least cost because doing so leaves them with the maximum possible means to buy everything they don't make for themselves. The means of determining this is the "opportunity cost," which is the lost income from not making any of the other possible products.

If a French farmer is growing 10,000 francs' worth of vegetables at a cost of 5,000 francs and could grow 50,000 francs' worth of wine at a cost of 10,000 francs, 40,000 francs is the opportunity cost of growing vegetables. Obviously he would be better off reversing the field. But he must also be aware that he needs to make a one-time capital investment of 70,000 francs to plant grape vines, and the vines will not be productive for five years. Assuming he has the capital to make the investment, or that he can borrow it, he must ask what his opportunity cost might be for that cash. Could he invest it and earn more during the five years than his deferred profit from changing his fields over to grapes?

If he could, then Ricardo had another lesson for us: The amount he can earn over and above what it takes to stay in business is what he called "economic rent." It is a measure of the strong demand for the land's product and the strength of the producer's market position.

In the long run, if open competition exists, a producer's economic rent will be reduced to nothing as more competitors arrive on the scene and put more supply into the market, driving down prices. The farmer may eventually get no more than 15,000 francs for his wine—yielding the same profit as the vegetables.

People should concentrate on doing what they are good at and can afford to do and use the money they earn to buy the other things they need. It's not so easy, however, to counsel an entire nation to do what it's best suited to do. Nations are full of people who don't like doing those things or who have been trained to do something else

that isn't as profitable. English winemakers and French sheep farmers will be put out of work if Ricardo is allowed to rule. Or, in
Ricardo's time, English grain farmers and their peasant employees
would be displaced from the land if Parliament repealed the Corn
Laws.

The grain farmers' solution was to campaign for the preservation
of the Corn Laws, just as the American steel industry, auto industry,
machine tool industry, and even the microchip industry have agitated
for import quotas when their businesses were beset by foreign competition; just as Main Street retailers try to keep Wal-Mart out of their
towns. Indeed, Parliament did not repeal the 1815 Corn Laws until
1846. In response to a wave of civil unrest and hunger, the English
government at last perceived that saving jobs on the land was not as
useful as lowering the cost of bread for the entire nation.

Summary

Free trade helps everyone in the long run and almost everyone all
along, but the benefits may be small until they are added up across
the whole society. Protection is almost always good for a small
segment of society and bad for the protected society as a whole. Thus,
the Principle of Comparative Advantage, however well known and
understood, frequently falls before the onslaught of political economics. It often happens that a large amount of suffering visited on a
small number of people commands more attention than a little bit of
suffering widely distributed. Responding to the needs of one group of
workers displaced by foreign competition is politically more attractive
than keeping taxes low for the general population.

4

Capitalist Immigration Policy:
Tear Down the Walls

Immigration is trade by other means. Instead of staying home and working with limited native capital—or waiting for wealthy foreigners to bring capital to their native lands—immigrants come to new countries to exploit the productive force of abundant capital. The voluntary arrangement between the new employer and the new worker is mutually beneficial, just as voluntary trade between businesses and individuals is mutually beneficial. But even more than in the case of trade, immigration is socially disruptive. The costs of immigration extend beyond the parties who benefit, but so do the benefits.

We need to review some American history here. In some ways, we are repeating it today. From 1607 to 1920, Americans prospered on the labor of legal immigrants. Though every wave of immigration met hostility and social rejection from those already well established, the country remained legally open to immigrants. They could hold jobs, get educated, start businesses, and operate as economic citizens. They would become eligible for naturalization as citizens after five years' residence. (The naturalization process did have a gaping exception: In keeping with the racial beliefs and policies of the eighteenth century, only white people could be naturalized citizens. This continued in the law from 1795 until 1952. Free persons of other races, notably Mexicans and Chinese, were not barred from living and working in the U.S., but only their children born in the country could be citizens.)

In many jurisdictions, foreigners could vote in local elections even without becoming U.S. citizens. The U.S. censuses taken between 1860 and 1920 found that 13 percent to 15 percent of U.S. residents were born in foreign countries.

There was always some resistance to immigration. Some established Americans believed immigrants were putting American citizens out of work, overcrowding the cities, and putting undue burdens on public education and health. In the 1840s and 1850s, a political party emerged from a secret society to proclaim a nativist movement. As a secret society, members had been sworn to say "I know nothing" when questioned about their movement, which was anti-Catholic in general and anti-Irish in particular. The phrase "Know-Nothings" stuck to the candidates of the American party, which had a brief period of success in the elections of the early 1850s. The party advocated limiting immigration, requiring a 21-year wait for naturalization, restricting public school teachers to members of Protestant faiths, rejecting immigrants for all public office, requiring daily readings from the King James version of the Bible in public schools, and reducing the sale and consumption of alcohol. The American party split over slavery and slipped into history's dustbin, although its issues are still in play in American politics.

Asian immigrants were excluded from entrance into the country under the Chinese Exclusion Act of 1882 and follow-on legislation. The large contribution of Chinese workers toward building the transcontinental railroad and developing California was viewed by whites in California as a social problem, not an economic achievement. Starting in the latter part of the nineteenth century, foreigners who arrived in the country from Europe were sent back if they carried certain diseases or seemed "likely to become a public charge," but otherwise the country remained open to immigrants from Europe.

After World War I, popular anxiety about immigration and immigrants was fueled by a red scare about the Russian Revolution and international communism. In addition, unions finished the war years in a much stronger economic position, and they sought to restrain competition for jobs. The federal government shut the door on nearly all legal immigration in 1921 and concocted a quota system in 1924, excluding all Asians and imposing tight quotas according to the proportion of the U.S. population descended from each possible country of origin, according to the census of 1890—before most immigration from southern and eastern Europe. The effect was to choke off immigration from countries that had recently sent the most immigrants. For example, about 200,000 Italians a year had come to the U.S. between 1900 and 1910; after 1924, only 4,000 a year were permitted to enter legally.

The economic boom of the 1920s, the Great Depression of the 1930s, and World War II made it difficult to assess the impact of the immigration crackdown—it was subsumed by greater economic and political forces. Even in that difficult period, however, shortages of farm labor occurred in the West. To answer them, special guest-worker programs admitted Mexican immigrants, especially during World War II. At the same time, federal agents rounded up illegal Mexican residents. As many as 4 million Mexican residents were sent away during the 1940s, according to the immigration service at the time. How many came right back through the porous southern border is not known. Because foreigners were not eligible for the few economic relief programs that existed in those days, the labor market ruled Mexican immigration. In practical terms, it was a process of inhalation and exhalation. When jobs were available, Mexicans came to fill them; when jobs were tight, Mexicans went home or were deported.

Racial restrictions were repealed in 1952, but the quota system remained. After the Civil Rights Act of 1964, which prohibited discrimination on the basis of race, color, religion, gender, or national origin, the quota system looked like an outdated and embarrassing legacy. Congress removed the quota system and the Asian exclusion provisions in 1965. Sponsors believed they were ending discrimination and providing humanitarian opportunities; they did not predict the large increase in legal immigration that actually followed over the next four decades. "Family reunification" became the new standard for immigration preference, which meant once people gained entrance, they could bring in family members in a geometric progression. A person admitted legally could bring in a spouse, parents, children, brothers, and sisters. The spouses of the brothers and sisters could repeat the process with their parents, children, brothers, and sisters, and so on.

Much to the surprise of many Americans, immigration returned as a social and economic force in the country. The 1970 census recorded the low point in the percentage of foreign-born residents at 4.7 percent, which was less than 10 million people. About 800,000 were from Mexico. The next 15 years saw dramatically increased immigration, both legal and illegal. The flow of illegal immigrants grew rapidly after 1965. Some came over the Mexican border; others overstayed student and tourist visas.

The U.S. government passed new laws in 1986 to control the number of people entering illegally. It was a classic legislative compromise. First, it gave long-term illegal workers a method of obtaining legal status without first going home and waiting years for permission to reenter the country. About 2.5 million people took the amnesty opportunity and legalized their residence.

Although these persons received a relatively simple free pass, the other side of the compromise was trying to make it much more difficult to come to the U.S. illegally. Staffing and budget for the Border Patrol was increased by about 50 percent, and the agency was directed to work harder to apprehend people coming across the border.

A third provision of the 1986 law put an onus on American employers. Reasoning that illegal immigrants came to the United States to work, the government tried to make businesses stop employing them. The law imposed the first penalties for knowingly employing illegal immigrants. It had been forbidden for decades, but there were no penalties, no enforcement, and little if any compliance. About three-quarters of the 12 million or so illegals arriving since then are working nevertheless—some of them at more than one job. In some cases, their employers ignore the law; in most cases the illegals present forged documents so their employers can ignore the law with clearer consciences.

From 1986 to 2001, the flow of illegals actually increased. About 10 million new illegals arrived, and more of the illegal Mexicans already in the U.S. decided to stay because crossing the border—in either direction—had become much riskier.

Those who thought the purpose of the 1986 act was to curb immigration were of course frustrated when nothing of the sort occurred. This frustration raised passions about immigration, as did the spread of immigrants beyond the border states and port cities into nearly every part of the country. Immigrants' work held down the cost of construction, hotel stays, landscaping, restaurant meals, and dozens of other services. Such businesses prospered because their services were more affordable.

The 2000 census found about 30 million foreign-born residents, of whom about 9 million were from Mexico. The percentage of the population in the census category "white, not Hispanic" was 69 percent, down from 90 percent in 1970. Census enumerators presumably do not find all illegal immigrants. Private analysts estimated that about 10 million to 12 million illegals were in the U.S. in 2000, about half of them from Mexico.

Advocates for tougher immigration laws say the number has always been bigger than the official estimates. They estimate the U.S. had as many as 21 million illegal residents by the end of 2006.

The Economic Lure

People are coming to the United States from Mexico, Central America, Asia, and Africa—legally and illegally—because jobs here are calling them. Farm jobs, hotel and restaurant jobs, construction jobs—many millions of jobs in America cannot be filled any other way than by hiring people off the street, without asking too many questions about their legal status or the validity of their papers.

Chambermaids are as essential to the hotel industry as engineers are to the computer industry. Workers are scarce enough in many parts of the country that market rates for illegal workers are above the legal minimum wage. In prosperous cities like Phoenix, it's hard to hire anybody, legal or not, to dig a ditch or do yard work for less than $15 an hour—and that's cash money, equivalent to at least $20 an hour on the books.

In 2008, the people of Arizona were aiming to test the costs and benefits of illegal immigration. Local officials were set to start enforcing the strictest state law in the country against businesses that hire illegal aliens. This law included a mass invitation to busybodies: Upstanding citizens could lodge reports with county sheriffs and county attorneys when they suspected a business knowingly hired illegal workers. If an investigation verified the suspicion, the state would suspend the business's license for 10 days. On the second offense, the business license would be revoked.

This legislation may face a tangled future in state and federal courts, but the idea of it and the prospect of its being enforced prompted great apprehension in the Arizona business community, as it should; the state was apparently up to its knees in illegal aliens working illegally. The Pew Hispanic Center, which does research in the field, estimated in 2007 that 500,000 illegal immigrants were in Arizona, with about 350,000 of them holding jobs.

Illegals don't necessarily respond to the census, but by Pew's estimate they constitute more than 10 percent of the state's 3 million workers—in a state with an unemployment rate of about 4 percent. (In the prosperous Phoenix-Mesa-Scottsdale area, where 2 million people are employed, the unemployment rate is about 3.5 percent.) Put another way, there are two and a half times as many illegal workers in the state as unemployed legal residents looking for work. Arizona needs its illegal workers to sustain its growing economy.

Illegals may be clustered on the bottom rung of the productivity ladder, in jobs that require few skills, such as chambermaids, roofers, janitors, dishwashers, and farm workers. But businesses need these jobs done, and they pay well enough to suggest their importance to the state's tourist-driven economy.

A University of Arizona study published in July 2007 estimated the state's annual economic output would fall 8.2 percent if all illegal immigrants were detected, discharged, and deported—a loss of $29 billion. It didn't include the loss of output from businesses forced to close if they lost their business licenses.

Many lawmakers know full well that businesses need low-cost workers, even though unions and other powerful interest groups want to reduce immigration to drive up wages.

Arizona businesses scrambled to comply with the law and to improve their ability to detect workers with false papers. In large numbers, they signed up for the federal government's E-Verify program, a computerized check of Social Security numbers and immigration documents proffered by job applicants. The Arizona law required businesses to use the E-Verify system after January 1, 2008. Unfortunately for business owners and some legal workers, the data in the E-Verify system are frequently wrong or out of date, according to numerous reports from the Government Accountability Office and other researchers.

In the federal government's own experience, mandating the use of E-Verify is of questionable utility. A year after the Department of Homeland Security announced the government itself would use it to check people it hired, most agencies had not begun to use it. As of November 2007, only five out of 22 offices, bureaus, and agencies in the Homeland Security Department itself were using E-Verify.

Fearful Arizona businessmen with options, such as manufacturers, started moving their businesses out of state—sometimes even to Mexico, where they can hire Mexicans legally. Manufacturers can shut their plants, move their machinery, and reopen elsewhere. That option, of course, is not open to construction businesses, resorts, restaurants, retailers, and other service businesses tied to their locations. If the law is enforced effectively, those businesses will have to pay more for labor, possibly a lot more to attract workers. Their only escape hatch is to halt plans to expand and to trim money-losing parts of their businesses.

Foes of illegal immigration say it would be fine with them if legal workers are paid more and even better if illegal immigrants unable to work go home and take their school-age children with them. The taxes on 8.2 percent of Arizona output don't come close to paying for the immigrants' burden on schools and other public services, they say. This is arguable, and both sides have statistics to support their arguments.

Reflecting on the perceived problem of providing public services to illegal immigrants, some Arizonans were gathering signatures for an initiative that would legislate against children born in Arizona to illegal-immigrant parents. The U.S. Constitution, of course, declares that anyone born in the United States is automatically a citizen. Because illegal immigration did not exist in 1787, the question never came up. The Arizona initiative did not speak of citizenship; if passed, it would outlaw issuing birth certificates—a state prerogative—to children born of illegal-immigrant parents.

Arizona was not alone in trying to stiffen the laws opposing illegal immigration. Several other states had similar laws under consideration at the beginning of 2008, and nearly 100 communities in other states have passed laws requiring police and local officials, in addition to employers, to investigate immigration status whenever they encounter persons who might be illegal.

Others have taken a very different view. Most local police and government officials do not question a person's legal residence when processing them for minor violations, registering children for school, or providing benefits from government programs. Some states outlaw such an inquisition; most follow a "don't ask, don't tell," policy. Los Angeles, San Francisco, San Diego, Chicago, Miami, Denver, and Seattle are among the major cities that have adopted "sanctuary" laws assuring residents they will not be questioned about their immigration status.

An Unpalatable Menu

In Washington, the legislative woods are full of proposals for immigration reform. They include

A. Round them up and send them home. Don't let any of them get hired for any job.

B. Build a wall, especially at the Mexican border, so no more can come into the country without permission.

C. Keep close tabs on people who come on visitors' visas, to ensure they go home when they are supposed to.

D. Have a guest worker program that allows them to come temporarily but make sure they go home again before they get too comfortable.

E. Don't let them have benefits from public services, such as food stamps or Medicaid.

F. Don't let their children go to public schools.

G. Amend the Constitution so their children born in the U.S. do not have citizenship.

H. Have a guest worker program that qualifies them (or some of them, depending on their skills) to gain legal residency and citizenship.

I. Let some of the most responsible, hard-working illegal immigrants already here have a path to citizenship.

J. Let everyone who has made it here have a path to citizenship, unless they have committed a crime or unless they have taken public benefits.

K. Let everyone here illegally stay here, but don't let them have citizenship.

L. Tear down the walls, open the doors, go back 100 years, and accept anyone except criminals and people with contagious diseases.

Whatever the political advantages and drawbacks to each one, none has enough traction to win passage in both houses of Congress. Moreover, these ideas are not mutually exclusive. Congress can mix and match to try to find a viable compromise—perhaps offering easy treatment for those here and tough treatment for those who come in the future. For example, there's B+C+A+D+I: This was the "grand compromise" offered in the Senate in 2007 that called for border security on a grand scale, with hundreds of miles of fences, 18,000 new Border Patrol guards, and pilotless aircraft deployed to catch intruders. Then, illegal workers already in the country before 2007 would have a chance to qualify for legal status, but all others after would be deported. There would also be a two-year visa for temporary work, not to be renewed more than twice and only after a one-year sojourn back in the home country.

The bill was a complete flop. Instead of providing enough different provisions to build a majority by pleasing senators of various views, it provided enough different provisions to anger most of them. In summer 2007, the Senate leaders gave it up as a hopeless job.

A World Market for Labor

In manufacturing sectors of the economy, Americans import what they need and export what they make well. Disturbing signs, notably the trade deficit, suggest we don't make enough goods well enough to support our import expenses with our export earnings. We might repair that problem if we import more highly motivated and highly qualified people. Immigration, remember, is just trade by another name.

Immigration is not all about blue-collar workers. Our current system doesn't even give a decent welcome to the best and the brightest would-be immigrants. The H-1B visa, which is supposed to provide special consideration to engineers, programmers, and other highly productive workers in short supply, is capped at 85,000 visas per year. High-tech companies hungry to hire burn through that quota in one day, and then some Americans wonder why they locate factories and research labs overseas.

When foreign students come to this country's great universities to get a great American education, they get a diploma and then an invitation to go home. If the current system were designed better, a visa would be issued automatically to any holders of graduate degrees who have jobs waiting for them. Even more significantly, anybody from any country who graduates from an American university should earn the privilege of working in America.

Among America's economic competitors, the European Union has taken the most enterprising steps toward attracting qualified workers in technical and professional fields. Under a proposal expected to be implemented in 2008, such people from outside the EU can acquire a Blue Card work permit—like the American Green Card— if they can arrange a work contract in an EU country. After two years in one job in one EU country, Blue Card holders are allowed to switch jobs or even move to another EU country if they find a job. After five years, they become eligible for permanent EU residency. The United Kingdom has had a "Highly Skilled Migrant Program" since 2001, and the government was considering moving to a points program that would effectively welcome people with university degrees.

Some countries also put out the red carpet for investors and businessmen. Germany gives legal immigrant status to anyone who invests 500,000 euros or more in German businesses or starts a business in Germany that employs at least five people. New Zealand has a similar program, and Canada's may well be the most effective in the world at bringing capital and capitalists to the country. A foreigner can become eligible to live in Canada if he brings $800,000 legally earned in business or if he has $300,000 and agrees to start a business in Canada.

On the other hand, European countries have not been especially successful at assimilating ethnic minorities they've acquired since World War II. Third-generation Turks whose grandfathers came through a guest worker program live in Germany, but German-born children of foreigners were not made eligible for German citizenship until 2000. In other countries, former colonial subjects fill service jobs, such as Arabs and Africans in France; Pakistanis and Indians do the same in Britain; Indonesians are a significant minority in the Netherlands. These minorities frequently complain of prejudice and repression, while anti-immigration political parties have gained strength in most countries. More recently, Eastern Europeans have been moving to work in Western European factories as fast as Western Europeans have been putting up new factories in the East.

Immigration and Imagination

When Americans gather to discuss the economics of immigration, it's always April Fools' Day. Some of us like to kid each other and pretend we can hold back the tide of people with tougher enforcement of existing laws, or a higher, wider wall, or some other magical instrument to repress the human spirit.

Running against people who cannot vote is not a new development. It's one of the cardinal points of the American political compass. Just in the twentieth century, we could think despondently of chimerical campaigns against communists and fascists, against blacks and Asians, against big business and big unions.

The U.S. should return to the idea that its borders are open to all who share the principles of American citizenship. If we have to build walls to control immigration, taking in new productive citizens will reduce the pressure on those walls. As a practical matter, the nation should welcome anyone who has a job waiting or agrees to take no social services during the five-year naturalization period. Applying for welfare, food stamps, public housing, farm subsidies, Medicaid, or any other service would void the contract and subject the immigrant to deportation. The immigrant could reenter the U.S. legally only after paying back the benefits received. The acceptance of public social services during the five years of naturalization should be a disqualification for citizenship and grounds for deportation, but the U.S. should accept people who can pay their own way or who have sponsors to support them.

The exception to the social service rule should be education. Educating people is an investment in the future of America, and it pays dividends. Communities must make that investment because communities benefit if the education they offer attracts economically responsible parents. The debate must be over the efficiency and effectiveness of public schools, not over the origin of students.

Although millions of Americans are unemployed, most of them don't stay unemployed long if the economy stays healthy. And the millions of statistically "discouraged" workers aren't looking for jobs and yet survive somehow. Meanwhile, illegal workers outnumber and outwork both groups. It's time to treat these valuable members of our society with the respect and legality they have earned.

No country with a generous social welfare program can admit all comers, but our country should admit all workers.

Summary

In the outpouring of opinion on immigration legislation, it sometimes seems the critics on both sides are right. Amnesty will be offered to most of the undocumented aliens in our midst, even though we have to dress it up and lie about its name. So what? Either we do amnesty by law or we do it by ignoring the law. We will never be able to round up 12 million or 21 million people and send them "home."

No impervious border will ever be established. The Border Patrol will never have the manpower to guard the Mexican border, even if it hires a lot of Mexicans to build a wall and guard it. Unless we post armed guards at the top of a fortified fence, we will have more or less the kind of border we have now, making the journey arduous but not impossible.

A point system or some other method of qualification for legal immigrant status will help foreign engineers, college professors, and nurses, and it will help all the businesses that hire such qualified people. It will not help Americans who want to be engineers, college professors, or nurses because they will face more competition for those jobs here. But America will be better off with more people creating wealth here; better off than it would be if the jobs were sent offshore.

A new guest-worker system will allow several hundred thousand people a year to come here easily, but it won't send them home again after a few years. It will be a way around the wall, that's all. No immigration reform will stop those of low skills from coming for positions that are on offer by the millions—chambermaids, farmhands, busboys, construction workers, window washers, and other "menial" jobs not easily done by machine.

Those of low skills benefit the most from making the dangerous trek. At home, they are surrounded by other unemployed people of low skills; in the U.S., there are jobs for them and their productivity is amplified by capital, in the form of construction machinery, dishwashers, water heaters, electric utilities, vacuum cleaners, and all the familiar appliances. At home, they would be condemned to generations of poverty; in the U.S., they and their children can live safely, go to school, learn trades, open bank accounts, and start businesses.

Illegal immigrants will stop coming to the United States when the elites of their countries provide economic opportunity, social mobility, and domestic tranquility, or if the American democracy trips on its own fears and stops providing economic growth and the conditions for a decent life.

5

The Essential Elements of Capitalism: Investment and Invention

Where did our modern industrial society come from? It was not invented all at once. It was not imposed on people by outsiders. In this chapter, we pause for a brief look back at the changes that occur in industrial revolutions.

The proverb says that necessity is the mother of invention, but necessity prompts creativity only in desperate circumstances. All too often, there isn't time for the kind of breakthrough that would save the day. Invention is more often a grim step-by-step process of trial and error in an industrial laboratory. Most important creations follow Thomas Edison's process, "1 percent inspiration and 99 percent perspiration." Recall that to develop a practical electric light bulb, Edison tried thousands of filament materials. Follow a pharmaceutical company through the tedious process of testing new drugs. Watch a software company manage hundreds of programmers, who insert thousands of lines of new code into an existing product and test the results over and over, just to get a few lines that serve in a new edition.

This kind of industrialized invention is a permanent cost of doing business in much of the modern world. This investment of time and talent is the mother of invention, and not just in the part of the economy that manufactures products. Ask a pop musician how many songs he had to write to get one that was worth recording or how long it takes to get a good track in the studio. Stay around after a movie is

82 A WORLD OF WEALTH

over to see the credits given to so many people in so many crafts, all
needed to bring the original inspiration to the screen.

We may give a nod to necessity and two nods to inspiration or creativity. But we should recognize that investment is the real mother of
invention.

Looking back over the last 200 years, we find that investment
powered the inspirations that created the modern world. The source
of British wealth was in its mills and mines, especially the coal mines.
Coal drove the steam engines that ran the mill machinery, pumped
water out of deep mines, and pulled railroad trains. It fueled iron furnaces and steel mills. Converted to gas, it illuminated city homes,
shops, and factories.

Better and cheaper iron and steel, made possible by large-scale
coal coking, were of utmost utility. Improved metallurgy increased
the strength of pumps, making deeper mines possible and creating
more opportunities for mining coal, which fueled steam engines built
of iron and steel, which powered mechanical spinning machines and
looms—and on and on as each improvement in each industrial sector
made possible other investments in other sectors.

Money and finance knitted together the sectors of the industrial
revolution. Profits earned in one sector could be invested in others.
Before the railroads revolutionized transportation in the 1830s and
1840s, the price of coal doubled with every 15 miles of distance from
the source. Immense profits in transporting coal funded investments
in bigger mines and in more railroads. Even though the delivered
price of coal fell rapidly, mining profits increased on the growing volume. Reinvested profits fueled a productive cycle of investment and
market expansion. At first, investment opportunities were limited to
those who already had wealth. Stocks in the most appealing companies, such as railroads, usually were issued for 100 pounds a share and
rarely dipped below that in the market unless the investment had
gone sour. The sum of 100 pounds, equivalent to more than $10,000
today, was completely out of reach for even the most industrious and

penurious members of the middle class, who did well to make 2 pounds a week. Even wealthy members of the gentry and nobility found it difficult to safely diversify their investments. Investing in only a few companies was perilous, as it is today. Construction of the early English railway system, laying more than 5,000 miles of track in less than 20 years, required an investment of 200 million pounds and produced the greatest stock-market boom in history. The boom was followed by a stock-market bust because it took another decade for rail traffic to live up to investors' huge expectations.

The investment trust, which we know today as the mutual fund, came to prominence in Britain in the 1860s. These institutions, which have become a key feature of modern finance, mingle the small savings of many small investors and hand the entire sum, minus a fee, to a (hopefully) knowledgeable investment manager. The manager then spreads the whole sum over a number of different stocks. The whole portfolio is more secure and the average performance, adjusted for risk, is better.

This financial innovation spread rapidly in the latter half of the nineteenth century and provided much of the capital that built European and North American industry. By the time coal and metallurgy had prepared the way for the next huge technological advance, finance was ready.

Electricity at first seemed like a curiosity rather than a major advance. It required an enormous amount of new investment—in generating stations, transmission lines, and a whole new installation of wires, motors, and lamps in every home and business. But electricity had several great attractions for industrial power. Electricity could be made with various fuels and with hydroelectric dams requiring no fuel: Generating technology could be adapted to local terrain and local resources. Electricity was flexible and scalable: Power-generating stations could be the right size for each local market, and yet a system could be enlarged as demand grew.

If electricity had merely replaced the kerosene lamp, it would have provided a modest addition to the Industrial Revolution, but it accelerated every aspect of progress by making possible new industries and ways of life. Household appliances gradually ended the commonplace hiring of servants and freed many women to enter the paid work force. The application of electricity improved the efficiency of existing forms of mass production, such as textile weaving, and created new ones, such as garment manufacturing with electric sewing machines. Electricity made aluminum smelting economically feasible. The availability of the lightweight metal pushed the development of the airplane industry from the World War I era of wood and cloth structures to its maturation in the World War II period of aluminum skins. Postwar airliners made international travel accessible to middle-class citizens of wealthy nations. Tourism became a major industry, broadening people's minds. New and foreign ideas were more easily accepted and more widely adopted quicker than ever before. Electrification and all it made possible opened the world and created the economic globalization of the twenty-first century.

The great engineer and inventor Thomas A. Edison gets all the credit for the age of electrification. Though he pioneered electric light and power and advanced electric technology in communications, transportation, and entertainment, his financiers made electrification possible. Edison did not invent the light bulb; he improved it so it could be manufactured cheaply and so it would last long enough to be worthwhile. Edison had the backing of J.P. Morgan and other Wall Streeters who knew him because they used his stock-market ticker machine. Edison diligently experimented with different filament materials. He eventually made a manufacturable light bulb that could last for more than a thousand hours.

However, Edison's greatest invention came after the light bulb. He created the system for generating, distributing, and selling electricity. In 1882, three years after developing an improved incandescent light bulb and exhibiting the illumination of his laboratory,

Edison opened the first electric utility. J.P. Morgan financed the venture, and the offices of Drexel, Morgan, and Co. were among the first customers. Edison built a generating station in lower Manhattan and wired one square mile of the city, serving 59 customers and charging 24 cents per kilowatt hour. (Today's Con Edison utility rates are about 5 or 6 cents per kilowatt hour, and, after adjusting for inflation, they are less than 2 percent of Edison's first charges.)

Edison developed a remarkably efficient steam-powered generator, devices for maintaining constant voltage, electric cables and insulators, light sockets with switches, and safety fuses to turn off power automatically in case of trouble. He even developed the concept of wiring parallel circuits so that every light was not dependent on every other light working properly. With the support of Morgan and his other investors, Edison started his own company to manufacture electrical equipment. General Electric became one of the world's largest corporations.

With technology well known and finance readily available, the use of electricity spread rapidly. Many different companies served small areas, sometimes even stringing wires in competition with each other. Many large industrial and commercial users of electricity even found it worthwhile to generate their own power.

Profits from electricity financed more inventors. George Westinghouse introduced alternating-current technology, and with it long-distance transmission of electricity could be a reality. Utilities could expand and centralize, using large-scale generators and high-voltage transmission lines. Westinghouse's transformers stepped down the voltage for actual use. Edison resisted the change, which weakened his Edison General Electric Co., but Samuel Insull would embrace the change and create the modern centralized electric utility industry. Insull had been Edison's business secretary until one of Chicago's electricity businesses hired him away. Insull moved quickly to buy up the competition, increase generating capacity, and stimulate new demand for electricity. He abandoned the direct-current technology that Edison cherished, and he substituted alternating current because it could serve a wide area.

With larger central power stations came a need for large and patient financial investments. Equipment was expensive, but it would last a long time. Financing utilities helped develop a market for long-term debt in the United States. The utility industry focused on growth, low rates, and slow-but-steady returns on investment. Insull's centralized power utilities were controlled by Middle West Utilities, a holding company, but the operating companies bought each others' stock with borrowed money, so Insull could control the power by controlling the holding company. This form of leverage was highly effective, and Insull's holding companies were the subject of huge speculation in the 1920s stock market—so huge that he warned in 1925 that prices were unreasonable and was quoted saying so in *Time* magazine.

Making such warnings did him no good when the crash of 1929 arrived. His operating companies lost revenues, but their costs were fixed. They went bankrupt one by one. Insull and many small shareholders lost their investments when the holding company went bankrupt in 1932.

Insull was indicted for mail fraud and embezzlement—political charges meant to mollify the small investors. After a noisy trial, Insull was acquitted on all charges, but politicians acted as if he were guilty. In reaction to the imagined abuses of the Insull empire, they legislated a set of clumsy regulations that banned most interstate utilities and most uses of the holding company structure for the next 50 years. Over-regulation and laws that fragmented the market held back the development of the electric utility industry because only risk-averse capital flowed into it, as a place of safe and secure returns, assured by the government in exchange for the industry's acceptance of state price controls. These forces also produced a generation of mediocre management: Only the least enterprising executives want to try their skills in an industry where outside forces fix the price and dictate a small but certain profit. Fortunately, the financial lessons taught by Samuel Insull's example, about the dangers of debt and the advantages of rapid growth, could be applied elsewhere. The quest for scale, scope, and productivity continued in communications, transportation, and manufacturing. America became a country of huge corporations and the world leader in finance.

Creative Capitalism

Investment is the work we do to create capital. Such work is scarcer than work done purely for survival; it requires people to recognize a future payoff for present labor. Even the lowliest subsistence farmer has to have some of that ability. Planting seeds now is wiser than eating the seeds. The seeds he sows grow up to be plants and bear fruit that will feed his family for months. But does he have the greater vision and ability to clear a forest and plant more grain? Or does he have the still greater abilities to use fertilizers, experiment with crop rotation, or cross-breed his plant varieties? And what will he do with his excess production if he has those abilities?

Capitalists break out of subsistence into creativity. They recognize that neither material things nor money are enough to create wealth. Commerce is the constant conversion of things into money, and money into things. Capital powers this dynamic process, a life force for human progress.

A depressing multitude of economists have been unable to distinguish between the accumulation of capital for productive use and the accumulation of wealth for vain display. Even Adam Smith complained, "The rich man glories in his riches, because he feels that they naturally draw upon him the attention of the world.... At the thought of this, his heart seems to swell and dilate itself within him, and he is fonder of his wealth, upon this account, than for all the other advantages it procures him."

But the rich man's vanities are also assets—created by his tailor, his grocer, his wine merchant, and his servants. They produce their goods and services to satisfy the market, which includes the rich man. They are doing no less for themselves by satisfying his vanities than they would do if they supplied clothing, food, drink, and baby-sitting to the most socially responsible schoolteacher.

Some economists, however, disdain consumption, especially conspicuous consumption in the pursuit of prestige. To them, all buildings are pyramids, all cloth is lace, and all cattle are sacred cows. By undermining the moral right of wealthy people to dispose of their wealth according to their taste, such economists and social critics have harmed the cause of prosperity for the people they wanted to help.

Many people believe that the production of permanent surpluses, indeed the creation of real wealth, is not merely difficult, but impossible in the long run. Thomas Malthus was one such, an early nineteenth-century economist who projected that the earth's food supply could not grow as fast as its population; hence, humanity is doomed to suffer occasional famines.

Following Malthusian thought, many classical economists of the eighteenth and nineteenth centuries thought that competition for labor would drive up wages and drive down the profit residual for the capitalists. They also believed that such prosperity in the working class would allow the poor to raise more children, and the population increase would enlarge the supply of labor and drive down wages once again. Malthus had opposed the Poor Law, England's mild effort to relieve misery, on the grounds that it would permit the poor to have more children, which would bring more misery.

But Malthus was wrong about the continued multiplication of the population and wrong about the slower advance of the food supply. Despite advances in medicine and public health that promoted longevity, birth rates declined and population growth slowed with nineteenth-century industrialization. Agricultural output increased dramatically everywhere, until England deliberately chose to import food from the United States, Canada, Argentina, New Zealand, and Australia rather than intensively cultivate its own little island. At that point, England became the first true industrial civilization. Farming remained as an excuse for the wealthy to have large estates, but it ceased to be an important source of British wealth.

The reality is that the combination of inventiveness and finance that powered the industrial revolution produced the first sustained improvement in the wealth and numbers of common people. Per-capita economic output in Western Europe was basically flat—averaging 0.14 percent growth per year—from the fall of the Roman Empire until the late eighteenth century. At that point, the average productive capacity of Western Europeans took off, even as the population of Western Europe also rose. Before that inflection point, economic output was linked to population: more people, more output. But output achieved for any reason, including technological advances, simply increased European societies' ability to expand population. The net result was that per-capita output remained at subsistence levels despite technological improvements. Other places were also ruled by this dismal condition, in which population growth canceled out economic growth. Peasants from Britain to China probably lived as well 2,500 years ago as 250 years ago. Conversely, tragic population losses because of war, disease, or famine usually led to a brief period of higher real wages and prosperity for the survivors' children. The children of those Europeans who did not die of the Black Death lived in the most comfortable circumstances any generation of Europeans enjoyed between the Roman and British empires.

In nineteenth-century Europe, the Industrial Revolution and related advances so powerfully changed society that per-capita economic output rose 1 percent a year. That may not sound like much, but it was seven times as fast as the average of the previous seven centuries, and over 100 years, even 1 percent growth compounded and reinvested will nearly triple the starting position.

The most important social change was that families started having fewer children. In the nineteenth century, for the first time in history, procreation did not keep up with economic creativity, and the mass of people grew wealthier.

The 1 percent per-capita economic growth rate of the mid-nineteenth century actually accelerated in the last quarter of the century because fertility rates slowed in the most economically advanced nations. The fertility rate in England and Wales peaked in 1871. In Germany, the peak occurred in 1875.

Technological progress plus declining fertility rates produced a per-capita economic growth of 2 percent per year in Western Europe in the twentieth century, despite two gigantic wars and the Great Depression in the first half of the century. Charles Darwin could have explained the declining birth rate. He said, "It is not the strongest who survives, nor the most intelligent, but the one most responsive to change." It seems that, because of technological change, the human trait of responding to good times by having more children became less successful for guaranteeing a lineage of descendants. It was defeated by the trait of investing more resources in fewer children.

The result of a changed economic environment was a greater pay-off to those who had smaller families. More investment in each child, especially more education, pushed the pace of technological change, which required more education, which made smaller families more economically advantageous, and so on. The results since 1750 are clear.

Never before was there such an outpouring of innovation. Never before was there such a restriction of fertility, so much so that, as it goes on, European countries face population shrinkage in the twenty-first century. Whether it's developed consciously or unconsciously, this change in perspective about the value of investment in education is the real take-off point for developing societies. There comes a point when even "unskilled" factory workers have to have some skills, such as reading and basic math. Children tending the looms in "dark, Satanic mills" are just not productive enough to be worth hiring. Businesses start to support taxes for public education because they need better workers. The deferred returns to a family's investment in education begin to outweigh the immediate returns to putting a child to work. Industrialization also raises the standards for public health, raising life expectancy. Parents need to have fewer children so that they can concentrate their investment on them.

Summary

Pessimism about prosperity and population growth was unwarranted. It has turned out that prosperity converts people into consumers, increasing the market for goods, and enough prosperity creates security and reduces people's desire for large families (even before the modern means of birth control invented in the twentieth century). But life in the days of the classical economists was punctuated by disease, famine, crop failure, and other disasters, so this was not an obvious mistake. Western Europe was more than a hundred years into the Industrial Revolution before prosperity trickled down to the lowest working classes.

Adam Smith's pin factory, which seemed a remarkable achievement to the eighteenth-century Scotsman, was only the beginning of the most important European revolution in history. Driven by technology, the change was not merely industrial. The application of water power, steam power, the factory system of production, railroad transportation, and urbanization changed every country in ways going far beyond economic output. Peasants left farms and became citizens, acquiring education, the vote, and economic power as consumers. They adopted new ways of life, new standards of comfort, and new manners of speaking and thinking, especially inventiveness.

Self-taught engineers made constant improvements in their machinery and their industrial organizations. The productivity of every worker rose rapidly, magnified by the application of more capital and more resources.

Displaced farm workers made their way to cities, where burgeoning factories needed their labor. In 1700 about 60 percent of the people in England worked the land. By 1800, 36 percent of a larger, better-fed population was employed in agriculture, and by 1900 the proportion of people working the land had dropped to 10 percent. In the same 200 years, the total population quadrupled.

The displaced people, however, found the process profoundly disturbing. They went from the poverty they knew on the land, where they felt in communion with the forces of nature, to an urban poverty working in factories to satisfy forces they dimly understood. A generation later the urbanized population would be far more advanced and comfortable than farm workers, but getting there was a disorienting struggle for those who were forced to make the trip.

As this process changed England, it eventually changed all of Europe, the United States, and Japan. It is currently changing China and India.

6

The Capitalist Take on Taxes:
Keep Taxes Low and Equal

A rashly idealistic man named Oliver Wendell Holmes, Jr. said that "taxes are what we pay for a civilized society." That was before the United States had an income tax, but the Internal Revenue Service liked that line so much it chiseled the words in stone on its headquarters in Washington, D.C., where the words shame resentful taxpayers to this day. The price is a good deal higher than Holmes could have imagined in 1904, and society has become much less civilized than it was back then.

One third of national income is taken in taxes. A research and lobbying group called the Tax Foundation converts this ratio into what it calls a national emancipation day, known as Tax Freedom Day. This is the day average Americans stop working to pay taxes and start working for themselves. In 2007, Tax Freedom Day fell on April 30, two days later than the previous year.

The Tax Foundation divides the total tax take of federal, state, and local governments—just under $4 trillion in 2007, two-thirds of it federal—by the $12.1 trillion national income in 2007. Taxes take 32.7 percent of national income and April 30 is 32.8 percent of the way into the year. The Tax Foundation also calculates Tax Freedom Day state-by-state and reported that average people in high-tax states and localities didn't have their tax shackles stricken until the middle of May. The top five tax burdens in 2007 were carried by the residents of Connecticut, New York, Washington, D.C., New Jersey, and Vermont.

Tax Freedom Day calculations uncover the major hidden taxes, such as doubling the amount of Social Security and Medicare tax to reflect that the real burden of the so-called employers' share really falls on the workers. The Tax Foundation also adds an estimate of the consumers' share of corporate income taxes to their tax bill.

It is also true that average people don't actually have average incomes. A few people at the top of the income ladder have very high incomes, which raise the average for everybody else. Nevertheless, the average taxpayer gets off lightly. Rich people pay most of the taxes. IRS data for 2004 showed the top 10 percent of American earners made 44 percent of the income and paid 68 percent of all federal income tax.

The highest-tax states are states with lots of rich people and high tax rates. If the top 10 percent of earners paid the same portion of state and local taxes that they did of federal taxes, their national Tax Freedom Day wouldn't come until June 7.

How about the top 1 percent of earners, who enjoyed family adjusted gross incomes above $328,049? They had 19 percent of all income and paid 36.8 percent of all federal income tax. On the same basis, their national Tax Freedom Day didn't arrive until July 23.

The bottom 50 percent of Americans who filed tax returns in 2004 earned 13.4 percent of the national income and paid 3.3 percent of federal income tax, for an average Tax Freedom Day of January 29.

This is what people call a progressive tax system.

Squeeze the Rich

Oddly, if you really want to raise taxes on the rich, you should cut their tax rates the way Congress and President Bush did in 2001, 2002 and 2003. It sounds like a joke, but it's the most sensible way to read the results of the Bush years in U.S. tax policy. After the Bush administration and Congress reduced the top marginal rates, the people with the highest incomes shouldered a larger share of the tax burden because they made so much more money.

The total national tax take—collections of federal, state, and local taxes—hit a low percentage just as President Bush's much-denounced income-tax cuts were beginning to take effect. But after the take fell to 29.5 percent in 2003, it rose every subsequent year and was 33 percent in 2007. In part, state and local governments were raising their taxes. Of more importance, the expanding economy generated more revenue from income taxes, sales taxes, corporate income taxes, and social-insurance taxes.

Lower tax rates produced higher tax takes, by percentage and dollar amount. No major tax law changes have occurred since 2004, so this trend was carried forward. By fiscal 2007, higher economic growth and lower tax avoidance covered the loss of revenue from lower rates.

Lawrence B. Lindsey, an economic adviser to President Bush during the tax-cut battles of Bush's first term, diagnosed the apparent paradox: "Lower tax rates, particularly on dividends and entrepreneurial income, provide incentives for people to give up some of their previous—economically distorting but tax-efficient—behavior."

More simply, high tax rates are wrong—so wrong that they cry out to be avoided. Lower rates are not so onerous, so taxpayers are more likely to go about their normal business without investing in the services of tax lawyers and their tax-sheltering paper transactions.

A tax system becomes too onerous when the total revenue it collects starts to decline. In the late 1970s, economist Arthur Laffer drew a famous curve on a napkin, showing that both tax rates of 0 percent and 100 percent collect no revenue, and that maximum revenue is collected at a rate somewhere in between. Laffer, however, provided no scale on either axis of his chart, and the U.S. is still conducting desultory experiments to find the tax rates that can extract the maximum revenues from the citizenry.

In principle, a tax rate is too high when it begins to suffer seriously diminishing returns.

The best way to find out the right tax rate is to start on the other side of the ledger. Cut government expenses to the bone so that we need to raise as little revenue as possible. The progressive income tax has brought with it the governmental equivalent of Parkinson's Law, by which government programs expand to consume the revenue available for them.

Indeed, on the federal side of the ledger, fiscal 2007, which ended on September 30, 2007, was a record year: The federal government took in $2.6 trillion, of which the individual income tax accounted for $1.15 trillion. Just to keep the books straight, the other sources of federal revenue are

- Social Security and related items brought in $847 billion.

- The corporate income tax accounted for $367.9 billion.

- Excise taxes and customs duties—the source of most federal government funding for the first 150 years of the republic— brought in $85 billion (and wouldn't it be different if we had a government that needed only $85 billion to operate?).

- Estate and gift taxes raised $26 billion.

Add in some miscellaneous revenue sources, and the federal government's total revenue was $2.6 trillion (rounded off to the nearest hundred billion). Fresh borrowing of $162 billion from the public and from Social Security taxes that weren't needed to pay benefits evened up the ledger to carry spending of $2.7 trillion.

When Oliver Wendell Holmes, Jr. made his famous comment, federal, state, and local taxes were 5.7 percent of national income. They have been above 10 percent since 1925. World War II was fought with taxes that took 25 percent of national income (and with a lot of borrowing, too). The federal tax take has stayed above 25 percent of national income since 1950.

Such figures would astound Benjamin Franklin, who said before the founding of the country, "It would be a hard government that should tax its people one-tenth part of their income."

Tax Magic

Hold on tight: we are going to take a roller-coaster ride through the politics of tax law. And that sinking feeling you're going to have is from the funny budgeting that permitted Congress to cut taxes in the early years of the twenty-first century without facing up to their full costs.

In a set of tax-cut laws starting in 2001, Congress followed the Bush administration's proposals and cut the tax rate on dividends and capital gains, reduced marginal rates, reduced the lowest rate, increased the child tax credit, eased the tax treatment of married couples with two incomes, and set in motion a gradual reduction and elimination of the estate tax. To hold down the apparent costs of these measures over a 10-year horizon, however, Congress also made the tax cuts temporary. For the most egregious example, a 45 percent estate tax was applied to individual estates with a taxable value exceeding $2 million, as long as the person dies before the end of 2008. The estate-tax threshold was scheduled to rise to $3.5 million in 2009. In 2010, current law says there will be no estate tax at all. But it also says that the tax comes back full force in 2011 and thereafter, with a threshold of only $1 million. This allowed Congress to report an unrealistically low long-term cost of the repeal of estate taxation. The lawmakers played the same sort of game with the other tax measures. Most changes enacted so far in the Bush administration expire in the next few years. These legislative quirks in the tax laws were designed to force the Congressional Budget Office and other official analysts to minimize their estimates of revenue losses over 10 years. This disinformation made the cuts a little easier to enact. President

Bush, of course, spent the remainder of his time in office campaigning to make his tax cuts permanent, but the lawmakers, even the members of his own party, were unwilling.

The best that President Bush could get through Congress was an extension of the income tax rate cuts for two years, leaving the long-term future of the tax cuts to the president and Congress elected in 2008. What kind of a tax bill was that? It extended a tax cut, but it left the existing tax rates unchanged. Militant Democrats saw it as a whole new tax cut—mostly benefiting the rich, to boot. To militant Republicans, the bill averted an unwanted tax increase. In other words, the answer depends on where you establish the default setting.

To be able to talk sensibly about tax policy, we should agree on a default setting, which would be the normal or natural tax rate, in relation to which all increases are tax hikes and all reductions are tax cuts.

Some believe the default setting for the current year is always the tax system of the previous year, no matter how many further changes were built into the previous year's law. It's just as reasonable to say the default setting for the Bush administration was the system in place in 2000. We are often reminded that 2000 was the last year the federal government covered its expenses with its taxes, even though those taxes absorbed more than a fifth of the entire gross domestic product—nearly a modern record and certainly not one to evoke unmixed pride.

As good a case could be made for the income-tax rates of World War II and the 1950s to be the default setting; we could then say every tax bill for the past half-century is a tax cut. Or we might reckon from Ronald Reagan's 1982 tax bill or from the bipartisan Tax Reform Act of 1986. In that case, every current change in tax law is mere tinkering that perpetuates the large tax increases of 1990 and 1993.

Perhaps we should start with 1912, the last year with no income tax, as the default setting. It would be interesting if we could go back to it with a click of the computer mouse.

Of course, no generally agreed-upon default setting on taxes exists. Every citizen gets to make up his own. And no practical constraint exists on lawmakers setting taxes (or incurring debt to be paid by future taxation) wherever their principles lead them. If their principles cry out for greater spending—on homeland defense, foreign wars, domestic social programs, or any other need—their perception of a default tax rate will be high. They should say so straight out and take the consequences, as Senator Walter Mondale did honorably and explicitly in his 1984 presidential campaign. Unfortunately, honor and truth are not always politically acceptable, and Mondale led the Democratic ticket to defeat.

A better policy would start from the (admittedly arbitrary) principle that taking from any citizens more than a third of their incomes is unjust and should be unconstitutional. (Others might suggest a half or a quarter, a fifth or a Biblical tenth.) Whatever the share, spending should then be conformed to revenues, and not the other way around.

The Robin Hood Principle

Of all the cultural legends handed down to us from the Middle Ages, Robin Hood has provided the most enduring economic model. The familiar tale of the outlaw who robbed from the rich to give to the poor was crystallized in the Victorian era by the American author and illustrator Howard Pyle in *The Merry Adventures of Robin Hood*.

Pyle's version of the fable has it that Robin Hood was an outlaw who had killed a man in an argument. Taking refuge in Sherwood Forest, he found others—poachers and victims of injustice—who were also outlaws. Says Pyle:

"Even as they themselves had been despoiled, they would despoil their oppressors, whether baron, abbot, knight, or squire, and they vowed that from each they would take that which had been wrung from the poor by unjust taxes, or land rents, or in wrongful fines. But to the poor folk, they would give a helping hand in need and trouble, and would return to them that which had been unjustly taken from them."

Pyle's Robin Hood stories taught generations of young readers about the virtues of justice and generosity. They also taught that if the officials in authority are oppressive, they can be rightfully opposed. Their ill-gotten gains can be taken from them and distributed to their victims.

Latter-day Americans sometimes forget these details about Robin Hood economics: Robbing from the rich and giving to the poor is not automatically just. It is much less so when it is done by government policy.

Most industrialized nations, however, have enshrined a powerful form of Robin Hood economics in their income-tax codes. The authors of the progressive income tax, which is the largest revenue-raiser in the United States, were not content with the idea that people should pay taxes in proportion to the size of their income. They held out for the idea that people should pay higher and higher rates of tax as their income rises.

In the U.S., some who earn very little income pay no tax—in fact, a program called the Refundable Earned Income Tax Credit pays some of them a negative income tax. For 2005, the IRS, acting as an official Robin Hood, paid such taxpayers $38 billion. Then a basic rate of 10 percent was paid in 2005 on taxable incomes of up to $7,300 a year earned by single persons. After that, tax rates rose, on the amounts above certain income points. The marginal tax rate on income above $7,300 was 15 percent, up to $29,700; then 25 percent from there up to $71,950; then 28 percent from there up to $150,150; then 33 percent up to $326,450; then 35 percent above that.

These rates are not fixed; they are just percentages pulled out of the air by tax-writing Congressional committees late at night as they tried to finish crafting the latest tax law.

According to the Congressional Budget Office, the results are steeply progressive.

The lowest 20 percent of American income-tax filers, with an average pretax income of $15,400 a year, paid an effective federal tax rate of 4.5 percent. The next 20 percent, with an average pretax income up to $36,300, paid 10 percent. The middle 20 percent, with an average pretax income of $56,200, paid 13.9 percent. The fourth 20 percent, with an average pretax income of $81,700, paid 17.2 percent. The highest 20 percent, with an average pretax income of $207,200, paid 25.1 percent. Of them, the highest 1 percent of all Americans, reporting an average $1.25 million of pretax income, paid 31.1 percent of that income in federal income taxes.

Robin Hood's followers are alive and well in the United States. On average, the progressive income tax works the way it was designed. But it is unjust to tax a dollar of income differently depending on who earned it.

The Impossible Quest for Fairness

In matters of taxation, fairness is the enemy of simplicity. Those with long or wide experience know that taxes are always unfair to somebody—if not everybody—and they always will be. Plato wasn't kidding when he said, "When there is an income tax, the just man will pay more and the unjust less on the same amount of income."

The United States Congress has labored for almost 100 years to produce a fair tax code, with impressively awful results. Just about every line on every tax form attests to the quest, in which each attempt to be fair to someone results in a dozen new ways of being unfair to someone else.

Why, for one small example, did the national government finally decide to be fair to married taxpayers with two incomes and eliminate the so-called marriage penalty? The change was unfair both to married taxpayers with only one earner and to taxpaying couples who live together without the benefit of vows. Cynics know that soon the legislators will be back, seeking to eliminate the "singles penalty."

Because perfect fairness is impossible, the quest for it is a moving target. Some lawmakers like this because they like helping constituents in exchange for contributions and votes. Congress changes the rates and brackets, for all income levels and all sorts of income, in an effort to satisfy those aggrieved. Sometimes Congress simply tries to have it both ways: It frequently legislates two or more different rates for the same income, two or more different treatments of the same expense.

For example, there are two different income-tax systems existing side-by-side, and nobody but a computer can guess which one applies to a specific taxpayer. There is the regular income tax, and there is the alternative minimum tax (AMT). After the citizens or their accountants have carefully toted up all their expenses that the law allows them to deduct, the AMT rises up and bites them for following the regular tax law. In a twinkling of electrons, the AMT strips away almost all their deductions and applies a flat rate of 26 percent for the first $175,000 of gross income and 28 percent to the rest, if any, minus a one-shot deduction that varies a little bit every year. The AMT was originally designed to make sure all wealthy people paid at least some income tax. It has become a penalty tax levied primarily on residents of high-tax states because deductible state and local taxes are one of the AMT's big erasures.

The AMT is not all bad. It's a nearly flat-rate federal income tax that provides an incentive for residents of big-spending states to demand lower taxes. Except that the rate is too high, it might well be a better tax than the cumbersome system to which it is an allegedly unsatisfactory alternative.

The standard AMT would hit nearly 20 million people paying their 2007 taxes, but each year Congress legislates a large exemption, good only for that year. Lawmakers have been reluctant to take the heat for repealing the law, because it would decrease estimated taxes over 10 years by $500 billion or more. They also don't want to make people pay the tax, so they cover up the budgetary impact by doing it one year at a time. All estimates of revenues for future years supplied by the White House and Congress are inflated by the assumption that the AMT will take affect. The one-year fix that applies for 2007 income was estimated to cost $53 billion.

In the regular tax system, the process of using exemptions, deductions, and refundable tax credits to reduce or reverse effective taxation at the lower end of the scale is leading to a system in which only the rich pay income tax, and at rates so high they also deserve exemptions, deductions, and tax credits to offset the unfairnesses of their special circumstances. The much-excoriated tax cuts of 2001, 2002, and 2003 accelerated both these trends. Congress acknowledged the ultimate futility of the tax cuts by refusing to make them permanent.

What Congress should work on as soon as possible is a new, simple tax system—and a new resolve to let it be somewhat unfair in principle so as to be simple and efficient in effect. America needs a flat-rate tax, on income or on consumption, with the lowest possible rate and the broadest possible base.

Tax-Exempt Citizens

Nearly a third of all wage earners in the United States pay no income tax at all. About one-sixth of all Americans have no taxable income by the time they finish computing deductions and exclusions. Another one-sixth are in negative income tax brackets of up to minus 40 percent. Thanks to the Earned Income Tax Credit, they fill out tax forms only to receive a check from the government.

Is it fair for a class of working people to have a relationship with their government that entirely consists of receiving benefits, with no contribution required? Is it good for society to create that class, and with it a distinction between makers and takers?

Check in with Edward Gibbon, author of *The Decline and Fall of the Roman Empire*. When the lowest income group has invested nothing in society, when its only stake in the continuation of society is the continuation of social largesse, society is poised for decline and fall. Even if their tax money comes back to them in benefits, it's still important that they pay. Of course there should be a social safety net, but a system of cash payments to the needy should be kept separate from the tax system. Payments should not be automatic, and the system of payments should help people raise themselves up rather than remain dependent. All citizens should be conscious of the tax system taking its bite.

The lowest income group does pay one form of tax on their labor. All workers pay 7.65 percent Federal Insurance Contributions Act (FICA) taxes for Social Security and Medicare on their first dollar of income and every dollar up to about $90,000 per year. The direct deductions from workers' paychecks are matched by employers with money that could have gone to workers in the absence of the tax.

Social Security benefits, however, are profoundly skewed in favor of the lowest income groups. What looks like a tax is for them actually an investment, and the rate of return on that investment is the highest for the lowest-paid people because they get a higher share of their working income in retirement benefits.

The frequently heard complaints about tax cuts being unfair because too much of the benefits would go to the rich are based on the misstatement of a simple fact. No matter how you slice the numbers, tax cuts benefit only taxpayers. When the top 20 percent of the people pay 70 percent of the income taxes, almost inevitably 70 percent of the benefit of an even-handed tax cut flows to 20 percent of the people. A grand scheme for tax reform should replace the income tax entirely, substituting a value-added tax or a national sales tax or a consumed-income tax. One Republican candidate for president, Mike Huckabee, was roundly derided for claiming that the personal and corporate income tax, including the tax on capital gains, the estate and gift tax, and the FICA payroll tax for Social Security and Medicare, could be replaced with a single simple sales tax at the rate of 23 percent. He overlooked many details, the experts said. Others predicted recession, depression, or apocalypse from such a huge new tax on every consumer transaction in the economy. But the new tax would be paid from the huge income increase that would flow from the abolition of all those other taxes. Also, pretax prices would fall after the removal of mark-ups embedded in prices to pay businesses' income and payroll taxes.

A sales tax would be hard to avoid, producing new revenues from the $200 billion or more that's earned in the underground economy. (Small cash businesses would find it attractive to evade the tax, but large businesses would have to deal with vigilant suppliers and customers, not to mention IRS auditors.) For a while, at least, the sales tax might not be subject to the host of special tax breaks that pollute the current tax code and deform the economy.

The nation could also feast on the new productivity created from putting tax accountants, tax lawyers, and tax bureaucrats to work in the real economy. The single sales tax would also provide unprecedented incentives to save and invest in new production, both raising incomes and lowering prices.

A sales tax of 23 percent or more would have many advantages, if everyone would really pay it according to consumption. It would be big enough to be noticed, so taxpayers, rich and poor, would start to ask their leaders to prove they really receive value for their taxes. It would be high enough so that most taxpayers, rich and poor, would sharply object to increasing it without being shown good reason.

The Most Burdensome Tax

If we can't bring ourselves to take a chance on a sweeping tax reform, we should at least remove some of the most burdensome provisions of the current tax system. Leading the list of unwise burdens is the corporate income tax. Repealing the corporate income tax would distribute benefits to every profitable corporate producer of goods and services, their customers, and those who work for those companies. It would enhance investment opportunities throughout the economy by eliminating the double taxation of profits distributed to shareholders as dividends and capital gains.

The corporate income tax is designed to appeal to voters who think corporations are like people, only bigger and meaner. The tax ignores the creative power of capital: Reinvested profits power the economy; taxing those profits reduces the power of the economy. When an individual captures and consumes those profits, that's the time to tax them.

The corporate income tax is relatively invisible; every consumer pays it without knowing because it's built into the price of goods and services provided by the businesses that pay it. The corporate income tax is not even efficient: It is a dead weight on the economy, consuming resources and confiscating them. An army of government lawyers and accountants enforces the corporate tax laws, and an even larger army of private lawyers and accountants devises ways for corporate clients to avoid paying the tax. These are mostly rather bright, creative people who might have had productive careers. The corporate income tax forces the United States to do without the useful things these folks might have produced in another line of work.

In a House Ways and Means Committee hearing some years ago, a tax lawyer for a big oil company hauled in a six-foot stack of documents—the company's corporate tax filing. It weighed in at 150 pounds. The weight on the company was far greater. The company used the equivalent of 57 people working full time for a year to figure how much tax the company owed, and the effort cost $10 million.

Multiply this burden across the business economy, and you find that—according to IRS estimates—businesses spend about 3 billion man-hours a year in tax-related paperwork. The hourly rates for this kind of work are steep. If the average is even $100 an hour, compliance costs almost as much as what the corporate income tax brings in. This is not the only tax-compliance waste: Individuals spend a couple billion hours a year coping with their personal income taxes. It's mostly unpaid, but time is valuable to those who are forced to waste it dealing with taxes.

Visualize the full-time equivalent of three million people working to comply with tax laws. That's more people than serve in the U.S. armed forces. Think of it: We assign more people to protect ourselves from our own tax system than we do to protect ourselves from all foreign enemies.

This gigantic waste is like taking all the new cars, vans, and trucks that General Motors builds in a year and driving them off a cliff. It's actually worse than that because we are wasting people, not vehicles. All the people employed as tax accountants, tax lawyers, tax clerks, or tax-return software engineers could have been doing something truly productive with their time. They could have been creating wealth and opportunity for themselves, and their society would benefit. We cannot measure the lost creativity and lost opportunity, but we must not pretend it was never lost.

As important as getting the principles of taxation right is reducing the uncertainty caused by constant change in the tax code. We should resolve to create a better tax system and then quit tinkering with it for 10 years. No investor can estimate his profit when next year's punitive rate follows this year's tax incentive. A tax code should be carved in stone, not written on a word processor. It should provide even-handed distribution of tax rates, with few exemptions.

Beneficial Taxes

Some taxes make more sense than others. We should make it a priority to tax what drags down the economy. A small but simple example is the tax on traffic congestion that some cities are using to push cars out of congested streets. It was pioneered in Singapore in the 1970s, with significant reductions in traffic. London tried it starting in 2003, with some success. The first rate was 5 pounds per day per car, raised a year later to 8 pounds. In 2007, the enforcement authorities in London reported a 16 percent reduction in the number of vehicles entering the congestion-tax zone but no significant improvement in congestion or delays. The rate would have to be a lot higher for traffic to flow freely on the crooked lanes of that ancient city.

New York City, most of which was laid out in a grid pattern with broad avenues and cross streets every 10 blocks or so, might have more success. Michael Bloomberg, the mayor of New York City, got New Yorkers thinking about a congestion tax in 2007. He proposed charging a congestion tax of $8 per weekday on cars that enter the part of Manhattan Island below 86th Street between 6 a.m. and 6 p.m. (This covers nearly all the high-rent commercial and residential districts.) Cars already in the zone would be charged $4 a day to operate. Large trucks would pay $21 or operate nocturnally. Imagine taking a stroll on Fifth Avenue and seeing buses pass you, rather than you passing the buses. Imagine getting in a cab and paying for actual miles traveled instead of hearing the meter mark minutes spent at a standstill.

City planners say street congestion costs New York $13 billion a year in lost output, wasted fuel, and lost time in a city where time really can be money. Nationally, the cost of congestion may top $200 billion, according to the U.S. Department of Transportation.

Mayor Bloomberg could not push the Manhattan congestion tax plan through the state legislature in 2007. Congestion doesn't have a constituency, but every member of the crowd has a good reason for being in it. Also, opponents argue that the flat-rate tax will fall heaviest on those least able to pay it, and those forced out of cars will overcrowd subways and railroads, and some communities will become parking asylums, and enforcement cameras infringe on privacy, New Yorkers are already overtaxed, and so on.

Even if these objections are heartfelt, they are insignificant against the frustrating inability to get anything or anybody moved quickly in New York, except by subway. The city is strangled by its own people, suffocating in its own streets, and somebody must pay for more subways and more buses. (More streets and expressways is a geographic and political impossibility on the island of Manhattan.) Who else should pay but those who benefit most from having their cars and trucks in the city? If it's worth $8 or $21 a day to drive in the congested city, it's likely to be worth the cash and the noncash benefit of doing business or having fun faster than ever before. If it isn't worth $8 or $21 to you, then you can take the train or bus or stay out of town.

The mayor's plan had some problems. He pushed shamelessly to get a federal reward for doing something of local import and in the city's own interest: The feds give out "gridlock" grants, and New York City is asking for $500 million to build new commuter railroad stations, with parking garages, north and east of the city. Such grants shouldn't be given except where the benefits cross state lines. The city should be using its own money for such projects within its borders. If Bloomberg is right, and the tax brings in $385 million a year, that cash flow could support a multibillion-dollar bond issue for transit investments. Of course, if the congestion tax brings in $385 million a year, a somewhat higher tax could bring in more and sweep more cars off the streets. And a higher tax, and a higher tax, until at last we find a data point for the Laffer Curve.

Where is the rate at which this tax starts to produce less revenue? It's likely to be a lot more than $8, and the city should work the rate up toward that point, at least aiming for a level that provides a substantial extraction of revenue for transit and a healthy incentive to use transit, too.

The best aspect of the congestion tax is its purity: Nobody has to pay it. Anyone who does pay it is presumably receiving a benefit from using the streets he values more than the tax payment. And the benefit will improve as more vehicles are driven off the streets to make room for the most valuable trips.

The worst aspect of the congestion tax is the same as any revenue issue: the questionable presumption that the revenues will be wisely used. New York City government is no paragon of good management. Bloomberg proposed entrusting the money to a new independent authority, of which the region has more than enough already—some useful, some not.

The existing alternative to congestion taxes is to make our cities more unlivable, to drive people farther and farther out of town. Most American cities have been doing that for more than 50 years, and the ones that have done it best regret it the most.

There have been experiments in congestion pricing on highways in California, Texas, and Minnesota. Airlines, hotels, and many private interests quietly use it. But no city in the United States has yet tried congestion pricing for the right to drive in a downtown area. Higher rates for peak-use periods annoy all the peak-period users, whether the commodity is electricity, highway tolls, transit, or movies. Despite the obvious success of congestion taxes in London and Singapore, most citizens would rather be free riders. That they should pay for the problems they cause is a capitalist principle.

Summary

Tax protestors and tax reformers enjoy a long and honorable history in America. The country was created by people who didn't want to pay taxes to England without being represented in the English Parliament. They should have realized representation wouldn't make taxation a greater pleasure.

Henry David Thoreau, a quietly passionate opponent of the Mexican War, the Fugitive Slave Act, and the telegraph, refused to pay his poll tax. Eventually, an official came around to put him in jail. He spent only one night there because his good friend Ralph Waldo Emerson paid the tax in his name. Thoreau did not continue the protest, and he wrote what he had learned from the experience: "If I deny the authority of the State when it presents its tax-bill, it will soon take and waste all my property, and so harass me and my children without end. This is hard. This makes it impossible for a man to live honestly, and at the same time comfortably, in outward respects."

At the founding of the republic, Benjamin Franklin thought it far more likely that the United States would continue to levy taxes than that it would continue to be a republic. He wrote to a friend in 1789, "Our new Constitution is now established, and has an appearance that promises permanency; but in this world nothing can be said to be certain, except death and taxes."

If they could see us today, Franklin and the other framers might tell us their Constitution failed to secure the benefits of a republic. Or, as Will Rogers said about Franklin's famous comment, "The difference between death and taxes is death doesn't get worse every time Congress meets."

7

The Capitalist Struggle against Low Finance: Price Controls and Regulation Endanger the Free Market

For every problem that arises when people exchange goods and services, a market solution exists. Free participants in markets adjust the prices they charge and accept. When many people want something, the price of it goes up; when many people disdain something in the marketplace, the price goes down. In the short run, prices change to clear the market—to sell all the products on offer in accordance with their scarcity or abundance. In the long run, higher prices send suppliers a signal to produce more; lower prices send suppliers the opposite signal.

Every market solution, however, creates another problem because some people are priced out of the market. Some purchasers resent high prices because they have to pay more than they want to meet the price determined by supply and demand. Some sellers resent low prices because the market prices do not provide them with the profit they hoped to earn.

Contemporary examples include software businesses losing out to a strong competitor, renters in search of decent housing at a price they can afford, established airlines beset by upstart competition offering lower prices, newspaper companies who can't beat the price of free advertising on the Internet, and on and on.

A natural impulse motivates people priced out of the market to use some other force to tame or twist the offending markets, forcing the markets to behave as the aggrieved parties would like. They turn to the government, and in the American democracy, turning to the government has become a way of life. To manage markets the government can legislate price controls and other forms of economic regulation, antimonopoly laws and laws protecting established firms from destructive competition, trade protection, tax credits, production subsidies, and many other creative uses of government power.

Price-Gouging Disaster

When a series of hurricanes devastated parts of Florida in 2004 and drove many thousands of people from their homes, price-gougers swung into action all across the state to clear the suddenly changed market and ration suddenly scarce goods. Some hotel operators raised rates for people seeking refuge: Imagine a Day's Inn charging $144 for a room when a sign out front says the regular rate is $49.99 a night. Gas station operators raised the price of fuel to as much as $10 a gallon. Many carpet cleaners, electricians, tree trimmers, roofers, and other tradespeople raised their rates to clean up after the storm.

This was nothing special to Florida; price-gouging happens in Texas, Louisiana, South Carolina, and anyplace where a natural disaster temporarily displaces a large number of people. But in Florida, for every price-gouger, there was an opposite and more than equal price-fixer. A state law passed after similar occurrences in the wake of Hurricane Andrew in 1992 made it unlawful to charge significantly more for goods and services in an officially declared state of emergency.

The owners of that Day's Inn settled quickly, agreeing to pay $70,000. Of that, $10,000 went to about 50 hotel guests. The rest was paid to the attorney general's office for the cost of its investigation, and anything left over was donated to the state hurricane relief fund.

Municipal and county enforcers also got in on the game. A county attorney in the Florida panhandle sued some men who had come from south Florida to sell generators and gas cans by the side of a road at 300 percent markups. The City of Fort Myers hassled an electrical contractor for charging too much for repair work after one of the hurricanes. City officials backed off, however, when the contractor was able to show that he had always charged more than other contractors, before the hurricane and afterward.

It may be hard for their victims to accept, but price-gougers serve a purpose. The chance of making a quick profit on the side of the road induces people to bring gasoline generators to a disaster area. High hotel prices encourage early arrivals to double up on a room, leaving more rooms for latecomers.

The chance of charging high prices eventually averages out with the occasional necessity of charging low prices. Exorbitant hotel rates on the night of a hurricane may make up for the unscheduled loss of revenue from tourists who won't return to a disaster area for days or weeks. Did anyone see a state attorney general demanding full compensation for hotels' losses?

The way the market compensates for unexpected circumstances is imperfect and uneven. But the imperfect and uneven market produces efficient results with less difficulty than a battalion of attorneys general enforcing a book full of laws.

We should recall, however, that every storm also brings out thousands of volunteers who provide aid and comfort to victims. Many charge nothing, or much less than the traffic would bear. It's admirable, but it's admirable because it's voluntary. Economic relations without liberty are meaningless.

Permanent Price-Fixing

Going after price-gougers is idle work, not the least reason being because price-gouging only occurs in response to brief emergencies, such as hurricanes or other disasters. Prices also respond to longer-term problems, for instance a state of war. Governments nearly always resort to price controls in times of war, primarily because they also resort to inflating the currency to pay for wars.

John Kenneth Galbraith, the popular economist of the late twentieth century, got his professional start in the Office of Price Administration during World War II. Late in life, he recalled, "From the spring of 1941, I controlled all prices in the United States. You could lower a price without my permission, but you couldn't raise a price without my permission or that of my staff. I began with a staff of seven and ended with something like 12,000 or 14,000. Only an economist could be accorded that sort of responsibility."

Even an economist—maybe especially an economist—should not be trusted with that kind of responsibility. Controlling prices seems easy, but it always ends badly, with shortages and a black market, because governments cannot control the underlying realities expressed through prices. War does make things scarce. Wartime governments do borrow heavily and spend new money printed for the purpose. Prices do go up to reflect the lowered value of money. Passing a law to say it isn't happening is futile.

Price controls always look like the easy way out to politicians who imagine that markets that don't produce low prices are naughty markets, regardless of the value of the products traded. Hard as it may sound, prices people are willing to pay are never too high.

As futile, difficult, and unfair as most controls on specific goods and services may be, general price controls of the type that John Kenneth Galbraith administered are even worse. But they have been common, especially in wartime. The convenient excuse is that, under pressure of war, people panic, buy what they don't need, and hoard it, making goods scarce for others and creating shortages of war materiel. A more accurate description is that governments usually attempt to disguise the cost of their wars by borrowing and printing money. Price controls are an attempt to cover up the inflation that results from refusing to admit how expensive a war really is. Because price controls hold down prices, sensible people refuse to sell. The next result is rationing—also commonly an attribute of war on the home front.

Competition is the natural human response to price controls. Black marketeers and smugglers acknowledge inflation by charging higher prices. They get around shortages by selling things outside the law. Even when the public generally supports a war and cooperates (up to a point) with price controls and rationing, the war eventually ends, price controls are eventually lifted, and suppressed inflation registers all at once, as it did in the U.S. after World War I and World War II.

Authoritarian governments, however, imagine that they never have to acknowledge the authority of supply and demand. They order supply, and they ignore demand. The Soviet Union ran that way for 70 years.

As recently as 1990, collecting a fee for brokering a transaction in food or other consumer goods was a crime in the Soviet Union, and selling stuff on the black market at prices higher than those set in state-controlled stores was an even worse crime. The penalty could be 10 years in prison. Harsh, but not as bad as it had been. In the days of Josef Stalin, the penalty for buying low and selling high was a bullet in the back of the head. Such laws were part of the communist ideology of equitable distribution—share and share alike in everything, especially in the shortages that were the natural result of price controls.

Soviet citizens were accustomed to waiting in long lines for their daily necessities. Sometimes shortages were natural, in the sense that no bureaucrat had commanded shoe factories to deliver shoes. But frequently, price controls provided incentives for corruption: Whatever was being sold cheaply in state stores was of the poorest quality, whereas the good stuff was being sold out the back door at high prices by hoarders, speculators, and smugglers. A 10-year prison sentence, even the death penalty, is not enough to stop everyone from doing what comes naturally—buying low and selling high.

After 75 years of dogma, Russia began to recover from this pathetic ideological disease. The collapse of communism brought normal Western consumer goods to newly private stores charging whatever the traffic would bear. Russians learned that equality of misery is poor solace compared to the bounty of opportunity and choice that comes with individual economic liberty.

State of Emergency

Even in peacetime, irresponsible government policies may cause unwanted, unpopular changes in the general price level, and if a government is sufficiently irresponsible, it may try to cover up its mistakes with the bigger mistake of general price controls. That's what happened in the United States in the 1970s.

- The Vietnam War caused the government to spend excessively, and the Federal Reserve accommodated the spending by printing more money for the government to borrow.

- The dollar began to sink on international markets, and domestic prices rose.

- President Nixon ended the longstanding promise to redeem foreign governments' dollar holdings by paying them gold.

- The dollar sank some more, and domestic prices rose some more, especially food because the U.S. was selling a lot of grain to the Soviet Union.

- Oil-producing nations demanded more dollars for each barrel of oil because each dollar was worth less.

- Domestic prices rose some more.

- Nixon tried to halt price increases with wage and price controls, which caused shortages and dislocations in the economy.

- Eventually the Federal Reserve stopped printing extra money, interest rates rose, a credit crunch occurred, and a recession took hold, ending inflation by throwing some people out of work and reducing the demand for everything.

Any similarity between the Nixon years and the Bush II years is not coincidental. People make the same mistakes over and over again. The Nixon bout and another round in the late 1970s were followed by smarter growth policies in the next two decades.

Like most political leaders who preside over a period of inflation, the younger President Bush had no intention of debasing the currency. He may not have known he was doing it. Indeed, it had been going on subtly before he took office. Credit on easy terms had been available since the mid-1990s and had helped drive the stock market to record heights, even though the general price level did not follow. Curiously, the Clinton administration was not running deficits: Taxes on direct and indirect profits on stock investment in those happy days were providing waves of revenue, whereas political gridlock between a Republican Congress and a Democratic White House made it difficult to spend the revenue as fast as it came in.

President Bush's biggest priority upon taking office was to cut revenues, and he succeeded. Unfortunately, his military and security responses to the September 11th attacks drove up spending, even as public confidence fell, and economic activity began to slow. Rather than accept a recession, however, the White House, Congress, and Federal Reserve worked together to increase government spending and keep interest rates low. Of course, they intended to win the wars in Afghanistan and Iraq, and win them quickly, so the country could return to normal. Instead, the whole country enjoyed a five-year era of cheap credit, channeled through house-price inflation.

This kind of inflation seemed different from the previous bubble in the stock market, and it enraptured more people. Houses, after all, are particularly precious things. Homeowners regard themselves as favored people, and people with bigger houses are more favored. The size of a mortgage does not measure self-worth, but the size of a house makes a powerful statement to neighbors and relatives.

At the beginning of 2008, the housing and mortgage bubble was well recognized, but how it would work out was not clear. Signs of declining confidence matched the declines in house prices. Less borrowing and less spending were likely to lead to a recession.

With multiple candidates of both parties seeking election to the White House, there was plenty of loose talk about stimulating the economy to avoid the recession and about finding new sources of credit to support the housing market. The Federal Reserve stepped in to lend money to troubled Wall Street brokers such as Bear Stearns.

The capitalist solution to the latest crisis is simple but painful: Overextended homeowners give up their homes and go back to renting. Banks that lent too much on terms that were too generous have to take losses, on their books and in the market. Some have to go out of business or accept mergers with stronger banks on terms not much different from going out of business. Unwanted homes have to be sold at low prices, driving down the general price of real estate, even for people who did not participate in the general frenzy of real-estate speculation. Taxes might have to be raised at all levels, and spending that seemed desirable has to wait for a better day.

That better day will come. It would come quicker if the White House, Congress, and the Federal Reserve all would stop trying to shield the people of the United States from inevitable economic pain. Recovery on a sound basis, with less credit, less inflation, a stronger dollar, and lower prices can secure the nation like nothing else.

Nations have found such solutions in the past. Even those that lost world wars—Germany in 1918 and again in 1945, for example—rebuilt their economies on the foundation of hard money and capital investment.

Ancient Traditions

The famous Babylonian Code of Hammurabi, promulgated 4,000 years ago and revered as the founding of the first impartial legal system, is also a testament to the human fascination with price controls. Hammurabi set prices for labor and commodities and froze economic progress in Babylon for centuries.

Ancient Greek city-states set the price of grain, oil, and wine, the principal commodities in their trade and thus the ones least likely to have stable conditions of supply and demand. The Athenians had an army of inspectors and set the death penalty for disobedience, but the chief result was the creation of huge profit opportunities for smugglers.

Romans were generally more open to free trading—noble Romans disdained trade and did not care how it operated, so it operated rather well, and extremely well after the expanding Roman military swept the Mediterranean Sea free of pirates. But in 290 AD, Emperor Diocletian succumbed. In an effort to stabilize the empire, which was reeling after 50 years of civil war, he reformed the coinage and fixed prices. Of course, he got the prices wrong for the value of the silver, bronze, and copper coins. (Even if he had miraculously decreed correct prices in 290, changing economic conditions would have made them unrealistic in short order anyway.) Shortages and black markets followed automatically. The law was withdrawn, but Diocletian's name lives in economic history.

Price controls have been tried somewhere every few years since the fall of the Roman Empire, with the same results of shortage and black-marketeering. It is sometimes noted that George Washington's army nearly starved at Valley Forge because Pennsylvania had begun price controls, that one cause of the French Revolution was the price controls that made bread scarce and expensive, that the Paris Commune failed because of its refusal to pay the market rate for supplies, and so on into the twentieth century.

The most recent large disaster in America directly attributable to price controls was the California electricity crisis of the 1990s, when retail prices were controlled for the benefit of ratepayers, but wholesale prices floated free in a minute-by-minute market for power. Utility companies could not cope, and the state's biggest utility went into bankruptcy. The state effectively assumed its debts and borrowed more, but economic growth staved off what seemed like inevitable insolvency of the select.

As people grew in economic sophistication, some began to see that competition is more effective than government mandate. But this insight has been abused and turned into a movement to create government-mandated competition. It's frequently called the antitrust movement because American corporate law in the late nineteenth century permitted the creation of trusts, into which many companies could be merged to form monopolies. Laws against monopolies are still called antitrust laws.

In the game of Monopoly, everybody starts out just the same. Then by the luck of rolling the dice, players start to accumulate property and money. The money then is used to buy more property, while the property is used to get more money. Players with good properties prosper, and players with lesser properties can't raise enough money to keep playing. As players drop out, the most successful player gets everything, and the game ends.

Is that just like real life? Is it at least the way real life would be if no antitrust laws existed? Some people think life is just like a game of Monopoly, whose rules never change, winners are determined by luck, and losers declare bankruptcy and go off to sulk in a corner.

A person who played Monopoly for days and days during a summer rainy spell should remember better. He should remember that the same kid won a lot of the games. Despite the element of luck at the beginning of the game, this kid was always able to talk the other kids into making trades that helped him to put together a monopoly a little sooner than his competitors. He always had three houses on his properties when the competitors had one or two or none, and so he would always have a little more money to pay the rent when he landed on an unfriendly space.

It's true—he never gave the other kids a fair shake when it came to trading properties. If a player did not notice that trading away North Carolina Avenue would give him a monopoly, he didn't tell the sucker until it was too late, and then he would mock him. It is painful to admit it, but admit it we must: Monopoly, the game, is a game of skill.

Bill Gates is like that kid. He did not get to be one of the richest men on the planet by being nice. By all the accounts of competitors and associates, he is combative, arrogant, disdainful, and avaricious, even though he has given away a lot of his profits. He and the company he built are highly competent, too.

In the anti-monopoly case the government brought against Microsoft in 1998, one claim was that the company could have charged $49 for the consumer upgrade from Windows 95 to Windows 98. The judge who reviewed the facts declared, "There is no reason to believe the $49 price would have been unprofitable." Microsoft charged $89 because it made a marketing study that showed that price would maximize total revenues.

Is that a crime, or competence?

According to the diagrams from Microeconomics 101, marginal price is supposed to equal marginal cost, and if a price is higher than that, the company charging it may be monopolistic, if it has the power over the market and uses that power to inflate a price beyond reason. But what is "beyond reason"?

In the software industry, the marginal cost of producing another unit of a popular program is the trivial cost of allowing it to be downloaded via the Internet. The price of software tends toward zero. Indeed, many programs are free. From operating systems to applications, one can do almost anything with freeware that can be done on a PC with Microsoft programs.

Pause for a moment to admire the competence of a company that dominates an industry in which many of the competing products are available free of charge. Then ask what Microsoft provides that the free competition does not.

Microsoft provides uniformity. Microsoft provides safety in numbers, otherwise known as the network effect. The more computer users who use Windows, Excel, or any other Microsoft program, the more valuable the program is to them because they can communicate seamlessly with other users and more easily innovate using Microsoft's tools. Uniformity is a service the market hires Microsoft to provide.

The judge, however, found as a fact that uniformity was a barrier to entry, behind which Microsoft unduly protected itself from competition. His reasoning, however, was circular: Microsoft supposedly profited from its Windows monopoly while sacrificing profits to protect the monopoly.

In an American antitrust trial, facts don't have to make sense. The case can be anything the prosecuting attorney can convince the judge or the jury to see. Nothing is more crucial to an antitrust case than the definition of the relevant market. If the market is defined widely enough, substitutes for the alleged monopolist's product or service are always available. A railroad, for example, might have a monopoly on service to Chicago for farmers in one Iowa county, but a railroad to St. Louis might exist in that county and another railroad to Chicago in the next county. Building an antitrust case requires defining the market narrowly. The railroad is guilty of monopolizing traffic to Chicago in the one county, but innocent of monopolizing all traffic in Iowa. Take your choice.

In the original Microsoft monopoly case, the prosecutors led the judge to define Microsoft's relevant market as the market for software to be used on Intel-processor-based personal computers, thus excluding Apple PCs, Sun workstations, Palm Pilots, network computers, many sorts of servers, and other possible substitutes large and small. In the market for Internet server operating systems, Microsoft's operating system was second among four products. The judge waved his hand and defined the market to exclude servers. More hand waving, and he excluded more parts of the market.

It's no less valid to say that the relevant market is the market for problem solving, which includes mainframe computer systems, Internet-based systems, Apples, Palm Pilots, calculators, and all their associated software. Such a statement, of course, would invalidate all antitrust prosecutions in the computer industry, if not the world.

The antitrust laws are wrong. They are wrong in practice for hardly any monopolies have ever been effective for long except those fostered and protected by a government. They are wrong in intent, for they work against the consumer's best interests while pretending to provide consumer protection. They are wrong in effect, for they prop up weak competitors and perpetuate their mistakes. And they are wrong in principle, for they deprive owners of the use of their property and interfere with free commerce between free people.

A century ago, antitrust and related laws intended to control the power of great corporations limiting the growth and wealth created by the Industrial Revolution in America. The best way to be sure the second Industrial Revolution continues for many more years is to remove the shackles of that bygone era.

Incommunicado

Competition is a wonderful thing. Consider the competition for the title of the federal government's most clueless regulatory agency. The Antitrust Division of the Department of Justice usually runs neck and neck with the Federal Trade Commission because the two share responsibility for America's most inane political and economic impulse. They have to curb business monopolies and bring them to heel for the one true monopoly, the federal government.

Every now and then, however, some other agency takes a role in controlling monopolies, and that agency surges to display its own economic incapacity. For the past quarter-century or so, one of the most obtuse agencies fighting the grand fight against monopoly power has been the Federal Communications Commission (FCC).

Never mind that American citizens have hundreds of ways to communicate with each other; only some of them are protected by the free speech clause of the First Amendment. Congress created the FCC to regulate electronic communications companies that threaten to become monopolies, such as local and long-distance telephone companies (both wireless and wired); broadcast, cable, and satellite radio and television; and even some portions of the Internet.

The FCC enthusiastically attempts to decide unknowable issues. From 2001 through 2007, it pondered whether a media company that owns newspapers should be allowed to hold broadcast-station licenses in the same communities as the newspapers. It had considered such issues before because its political instructions are to restrict the potential for monopoly broadcasting. For decades, the FCC had said no company could have more than five television, five AM radio, and five FM radio stations. Then in the 1980s it said six, then ten. In the 1990s it changed the limit to a percentage of the potential national audience, and then it argued about setting the right the percentage. In a recent decision, published in February 2008, it reset the rules again, allowing newspapers to own broadcast stations in the same markets, but only in the 20 largest markets.

The FCC made such decisions in the name of the public interest, which is whatever three out of five commissioners can agree on, subject to review by the federal courts. Questions about who should own what don't have objective answers. Congress, which is careful not to answer them itself, hands the job to the FCC to answer them anyway. The FCC will never finish the job, for it is certain that Congress will keep writing new laws with new instructions to the agency.

The FCC should decide these issues by considering the First Amendment: Congress never should make laws abridging the freedom of any media, whether they communicate with paper and ink or electronics.

A chairman of the FCC in the 1980s named Mark Fowler, who was more interested in freedom than regulation, quipped that the public interest consists of whatever the public is interested in. Governments may attempt to impose finer standards, for example requiring radio stations to broadcast a certain amount of news, but they can't require the public to listen. Only unbridled business competition, with secure private-property rights, can provide both coherent services and the liberty to use the services.

Restraint of Trade

Unbridled business competition is sadly lacking, even in the United States, the world's greatest capitalist country. Even in one of that nation's most successful and important industries, competition is bridled, but not thoroughly enough to suit every powerful interest.

A pill to hold down blood pressure, be it ever so dear, is far less expensive than a triple-bypass operation or a stay in intensive care after a heart attack. The reason Americans spend so much on drugs—

more than 15 percent of all money spent on health care—is not that rapacious manufacturers must be satisfied. The reason is that drugs work, and many drugs work wonders. They are the cheapest form of health care by far.

Drug prices that ran up twice as fast as inflation during the 1980s and 1990s may well have been the biggest bargain in the history of health care, and a bargain that keeps on saving, because most drug companies reinvested a healthy share of their profits in the quest for more new drugs.

But the drug price controls contained in every bid for health-care "reform" would reduce those profits in a pure demonstration of the power of politics to restrain capital.

Price controls are foolish, but especially for an industry in the throes of technological and economic change. Biotechnology is only part of the change reconstructing the pharmaceutical industry. New techniques in lab biology and chemical manufacturing also have brought the day of designer drugs closer. Rather than examining compounds to see what disease they might fight, pharmaceutical engineers sometimes can define the characteristics of compounds that might fight a specific disease. Although this is far from infallible, it narrows the search for effective drugs and makes dramatic breakthroughs more likely.

Technological changes produce economic changes. The research-driven pharmaceutical house—dispersed across international boundaries and biological territories and creating, manufacturing, and distributing a whole portfolio of drugs—may be on the way out. What IBM and Digital Equipment discovered about the computer industry may soon be unveiled for the pharmaceutical industry: Playing it bureaucratically safe and attempting to manage the pace of change and profit is more dangerous than taking obvious risks.

What can replace pharmaceutical giants? Manufacturing specialists, growing out of the generic-drug industry; research specialists, growing out of the biotechnology industry; distribution specialists, growing out of the marketing department of the old industry. Large, established research pharmaceutical corporations may be able to hold their own, but a move to specialization is already taking place. Companies strong in research are combining forces. Companies strong in manufacturing are setting up their own generic subsidiaries. Companies strong in marketing are broadening their scope through acquisitions.

All this change can be stopped in its tracks with price controls, which would convert a dynamic industry into a dull public utility. In free markets, drug-industry economics are changing. Even without any far-reaching government reform, people by the millions have joined health maintenance organizations, preferred-provider organizations, and other forms of prepaid medical coverage. These organizations, in turn, negotiate with health-care providers, including drug companies, for volume discounts. Far from a monopolistic industry, pharmaceuticals have become a hotly competitive bazaar. Prices vary widely as new deals are struck. Of course, a good wind blows somebody ill. When prices are negotiated according to the economic strength of the purchaser, the weakest buyers pay the highest prices.

If they have any utility, price controls might produce an invigorated quest for new blockbusters because the clear-cut demand for a new cure would overwhelm any attempt to distort the supply. Could any national price authority dare withhold a cure for cancer on the grounds of excessive cost? Unfortunately, observable behavior by companies points in the opposite direction. Companies based in countries with rigorous price controls, such as France, Italy, and Japan, tend to concentrate on local copies of internationally successful drugs. Breakthrough drugs disproportionately originate in countries with the lightest regulation of prices of new drugs, such as the U.S., Germany, Switzerland, Britain, and the Netherlands.

Does this mean, as the pharmaceutical industry claims, that the profit motive drives research and innovation? Either that or companies with high profits have more investable cash floating around. One sounds nobler than the other, although either way it's money that makes the mare go.

Summary

America must rediscover the utility of prices that reflect "all the traffic can bear" rather than the least a manufacturer can afford to charge. Fixing prices restricts supply and causes shortages. It cripples innovation and progress. When manufacturers make high profits from high prices, they are more likely to plow those profits back into the quest for other highly profitable goods, whether the goods are wrinkle-free trousers, microprocessors, or life-saving medications.

8

A Capitalist Diagnosis for the High Cost of Health Care: Pay What It's Worth

Can such a thing as a universal, affordable, high-quality health-care system exist? Most "realists" say you can have any two of these attributes, but not all three at the same time. Such realists are actually optimists: Building a system that accomplishes more than one of these three goals might be impossible.

Most universal systems are turning out to be unaffordable in the long run to the economies that support them. All across Europe, governments are trying to hold down the rapidly rising cost of their universal health-care programs. The number of things that medical science can do keeps growing, and many of the new things are more expensive than doing nothing used to be. To save money, universal systems limit available drugs and treatments or force patients to wait for them. A slow, systemwide decline in quality is the natural result.

Most affordable systems aren't universal: They don't cover the most expensive illnesses or the cost of long-term care for the aged— or they scrimp on the quality or timeliness of the care, or both.

Quality is in the eye of the beholder: Health-care systems everywhere, whether private or governmental, fudge their self-imposed standards of quality to cover more people or to lower the cost to the government.

At a more basic level, each of these high-sounding values has a flip side: Universal also means compulsory; affordable also means price controls; high quality also means expensive.

In the United States, which has never had universal government
health care, we have experienced all the problems associated with universal health care and few of the benefits.

American problems with health care include high spending, rapidly growing higher, and questionable quality of care, even though the
system fails to provide for large numbers of uninsured and underin-
sured people. American politicians are advocating a range of fixes,
including tax credits, savings incentives, government mandates to be
insured, new programs to provide health insurance or health care to
everyone, and extending existing programs. None of these strategies
commands a majority across the interested groups, which include
consumers, health-care providers, insurers, employers who pay for
health insurance, employers who don't pay for health insurance, and,
most importantly, lawmakers. The status quo seems to be everyone's
second choice, so that's what we get.

At $2.3 trillion in a $14 trillion economy, the per-capita cost of
American health care is the highest in the world, but even that's not
high enough to do everything Americans want it to do. They want
health care everyone can afford, and they want as much health care as
everyone can consume—cradle to grave, with emphasis on putting off
death as long as possible.

Refusing to recognize this, the authors of reform plans have
promised that they won't drive up the total cost of American health
care—which means they must rearrange it. Rearranging costs and
benefits means creating winners and losers—and uncertainty. Interested parties will not support a plan that does not obviously improve
their own situations. To everyone, except the minority of people gambling with their lack of health insurance, the status quo is more comfortable than gambling on reform.

A Century of Failed Reform

Assuming we want universal, affordable, high-quality health care, do we really want a compulsory, price-controlled, high-cost health-care system? Aren't we already too close to that? Universal, affordable, high-quality health care is an obvious political winner in the abstract, and so the twentieth century saw seven major presidential efforts to enact an American plan:

- Theodore Roosevelt and the American Medical Association tried to create universal health-insurance plans state by state during the first eight years of the 1900s.

- Some of Franklin D. Roosevelt's most ardent New Dealers sought to include national health insurance as part of Social Security in the 1930s.

- Harry S. Truman renewed the struggle in the 1940s but could not get his national health plan through Congress.

- Lyndon B. Johnson's Great Society enactments of Medicare (universal health care for people over 65 years old) and Medicaid (universal health care for impoverished people) in 1965 were the only victories for the cause.

- Richard M. Nixon proposed mandatory employer-paid insurance in 1971 to cover catastrophic health expenses. He also proposed extension of Medicaid to all those not employed.

- Jimmy Carter reformulated Truman's plan in 1978, but his proposal could not compete with an energy crisis for Congressional attention.

- The 1993 "managed-competition" proposal of Bill Clinton's administration combined Truman and Nixon, with some differences in the details. It fell to intense opposition from the health and insurance industries, which would have had to deal with the expense of its complex system of economic subsidies and penalties.

Underneath this lack of political progress, the private health-insurance industry was growing, and it now covers more than half of all Americans: About 150 million are covered by employer-sponsored health-care programs, and about 25 million more pay as individuals.

Despite tallying only one victory among the attempts of seven administrations, the government side of the health-care system grew anyway. The federal government subsidizes employer-sponsored programs with a tax deduction (but there is no deduction for individual premium payments). More directly, using a payroll tax and general revenues, it pays most Medicare expenses for 40 million elderly and disabled people. Another 40 million very poor people are on Medicaid, whose costs are shared by states and the federal government.

More than 47 million Americans have no insurance, so when they seek care they go to hospital emergency rooms and public health clinics. Those institutions pass on what they can to Medicare and Medicaid if the patients are eligible, and then they build the cost of uncompensated care into the service charges they bill to all payers.

As complex as this description of our health-care system may sound, it is actually much more complicated. To sort out what is public and what is private in the health-care system is to invite a never-ending argument. More than half of Americans are in private health-care plans, but more than half the money spent on health care is tax money.

Americans spend about 15.3 percent of the gross domestic product (GDP) on health care—more than any other country. And more than 90 percent of health care delivered to American patients is paid for by somebody else—an insurer, an employer, or the government. Most patients incur only small cash charges compared to the price of their care. They do pay, but indirectly through payroll taxes, lower wages, higher income and sales taxes, higher prices for goods and services, and higher interest rates.

The national slogan for the existing American health-care system should be "This Is Not a Bill," which is imprinted on so many statements from health-care providers. The confused recipients are invited to believe they're getting something for nothing.

Can't we imagine another system—a system in which we pay directly for what we get and know what we are getting?

One popular health care reform proposal might seem to qualify, but it doesn't: A single-payer system of national health insurance pays all charges. Even simpler, a national health service can own all health-care institutions and employ all health-care providers. In these systems, citizens pay the government to make all health-care decisions for them. To a growing number of major employers, the prospective benefits of a national health-insurance system are starting to outweigh the costs. Ford and General Motors are joining the United Auto Workers union in support of the idea. They have noticed how much less of a direct health-care burden their Canadian employees and retirees are than their U.S. employees and pensioners. Perhaps they haven't noticed that taxes are higher in Canada, in part because of the cost of Canadian provincial health-care systems.

In 2006, the Maryland state legislature passed a law forcing employers with more than 10,000 employees in the state to spend at least 8 percent of wage costs on employee health benefits or make a "contribution" of the same size to the state's Medicaid plan for the poor. Wal-Mart was the only employer in the state affected by the law. Wal-Mart is unpopular among some politicians because it is resolutely antiunion and among some business circles because its low prices are hard to compete against. The state legislators who sponsored the law played on both resentments, but they did not say why they had singled out Wal-Mart on the basis of size, when smaller companies with better profit margins don't pay 8 percent for employee health insurance.

This gave Wal-Mart a reason to look at national health insurance, which may have been part of the Maryland legislature's point. Other states are considering similar action, and if it becomes a trend, all

employers with less-than-generous health-care benefits will see that
they could be next.

This is a new way of looking at the health-care issue—not as a
crusade to extend a new right to all Americans, but as redistributing a
huge burden that makes U.S. industries less competitive. As such,
national health insurance is also gaining new adherents in small businesses, where health care's share of labor cost often retards the creation of new and productive jobs.

Massachusetts took a different tack. In 2006, the state passed a
law to make health insurance mandatory but also to make it affordable. The basic idea was to permit insurance companies to offer
cheap policies with limited coverage and high deductibles. They
cover hospitalization and other expensive treatments, relieving hospitals and private insurance of the bulk of their bad debts and relieving
Medicaid of some of its expenses. The new plan also needed new
money, and here the state applied the Maryland example: It levied a
$295-per-employee "pay-or-play" tax on employers that don't offer
health insurance as a fringe benefit. It didn't focus on Wal-Mart, but
it did exempt businesses with 10 or fewer employees.

The Massachusetts plan was flawed because many people on the
bare minimum policies weren't able to afford routine care and pre-
ventive care. Penalizing businesses that decide not to provide health
insurance was not a step in the direction of individual responsibility.
The employee limit to favor small businesses also created a large
penalty for adding an eleventh employee—penalizing business success. The requirement for all persons to have at least the minimum
health insurance lacked teeth. The penalty for being caught disobey-
ing was only half the projected cost of the minimum insurance.

Even admirers of the Massachusetts plan have been disappointed
since its enactment. The penalty for ignoring the mandate was
watered down to a vague threat to take away tax refunds. Without
enforcing a mandate to pay, the parallel state mandate to write insurance for all must collapse in a heap of adverse selection—some don't

buy insurance until they need it, which raises the price for those who do buy it. A year after enactment, more than half the uninsured people of the state had not bought their health insurance. The state also confronted much higher costs than expected in its original projections.

Caring about Health Care

Insured Americans never have cared much about the uninsured—that's why six out of seven political health-care movements in the twentieth century never took hold. But every troubled company starts its restructuring by raising health-insurance charges and cutting retiree health care, so Americans do care about themselves and about not joining the ranks of the uninsured. Saving ourselves by saving employers through creation of a national health-care system could become an unstoppable movement whenever such worries become dominant.

It is possible that the U.S. could afford a British- or Canadian-style system without drawbacks. At least it should be possible. According to the Organisation for Economic Co-operation and Development (OECD), the U.S. spends twice as much per person on health care as any of the developed countries in Europe. The U.S. also spends a greater percentage of its GDP on health care.

Among the larger industrial countries in 2005, Canada spent 9.8 percent of GDP on health care; the U.K. 8.3 percent; France 11.1 percent; Germany 10.7 percent; and Japan 8 percent. The U.S. spent 15.2%. The differences are even more striking when spending per capita is compared: The U.S. spent $6,401 per person, and 45 percent of the money spent was government funds; Canada spent $3,326 per person, and 70 percent was government funds; the U.K. spent $2,724 per person, and 87 percent was government funds; France spent $3,374 per person, and 80 percent was government funds; Germany spent $3,287 per person, and 76 percent was government funds; and Japan spent $2,358 per person, and 81 percent was government funds.

Putting together the spending and the government share reveals an interesting fact, rarely noted in the American debate on health-care policy: Government health-care spending is similar among all the countries. Governments in the U.S. spent $2,880 per person on health care in 2005. In Canada, the government spent $2,328; in Britain, $2,369; in France, $2,699; in Germany, $2498; in Japan, $1,909.

The extra spending that pushes the U.S. into the top rank of total per-capita spending is private spending, as might be expected for a country that relies so heavily on employer-sponsored health insurance. All this spending, however, does not produce better results. U.S. life expectancy at birth is a year or two less than Japan, Canada, and the countries of Western Europe. The other countries also report somewhat better life expectancies for persons age 65, though the difference isn't as great.

What are the chances of enacting a U.S. health-insurance system that divides the amount the government spends among more people— in effect reducing the government-financed health-care benefits for people who have health insurance? About zero. Or the alternative: What are the chances of enacting a national health-insurance system that raises the tax burden by $3,520 for every person in the country, a total of about $1 trillion? Not much better than zero.

This explains why American advocates of national health insurance or national health care have had so little success: The large majority of people who already have insurance or government benefits would lose either some coverage or pay more money for the same coverage.

The Frightening Future

The amount of money that American taxpayers spend on health care is due to rise substantially in the next few decades with no change in law. Medicare pays for health care for the elderly and disabled, and its health care costs have been rising at a far faster rate than its covered population—which is rising rapidly anyway with the graying of the baby-boomer generation. Beneficiaries pay some of the cost of Medicare hospitalization insurance, physicians' services coverage, and prescription-drug coverage, but the federal government pays most of it, and about half comes from general revenue and borrowing, not from the Medicare payroll tax. Official estimates say Medicare's hospital-insurance cost will rise from the current level of 1.4 percent of GDP to 5 percent in 2081. Physicians' services outlays were 1.3 percent of GDP in 2006 and are projected to grow to about 4 percent by 2081. (This could easily be 5 percent of GDP; the 4 percent figure reflects unrealistic reductions in physician payments required under current law.) Prescription-drug outlays are estimated to rise from 0.4 percent of GDP in 2006 to about 2.4 percent by 2081.

Add it up, and we see Medicare costs rising from 3.1 percent of GDP ($408 billion) to 6.6 percent of GDP in 2030 and 11.3 percent of GDP in 2081.

A drastic reform of health-care financing in the U.S. probably requires a drastic reform of health-care practice. The U.S. has fewer physicians per capita than most other developed countries—2.4 physicians per 1,000 people in the U.S. versus the OECD average of 3 physicians. The U.S. also has fewer nurses, fewer hospital beds, shorter patient stays in hospitals, and more outpatient surgeries.

Some public-health measures are working in the U.S. Through high taxes, advertising bans, and relentless public-information campaigns, the U.S. has cut the rate of smoking to the second lowest among OECD countries.

Others measures are not working: The U.S. has the highest obesity rate in the OECD.

The Wizard of Health Care

Think of universal health care as the Emerald City Health-Care Plan, in which we must never look behind the curtain to see what makes it work.

Most ideas for national health insurance in America include some form of price controls on drugs, just as they do in countries that already have a national health-care system. Thinking that price controls could improve health is dangerous. Price controls, as we ought to know, constrict supply and choke off innovation. When we are sick in 2030, we will not want to be limited to the pharmacology of 2007.

In the days of L. Frank Baum, author of *The Wizard of Oz*, Americans had a different image of physicians than today's reality. General practitioners visited their patients at home. They set broken bones or let fevers run their course. Nineteenth-century doctors had plenty of time for house calls because they hardly could cure anything, as their patients knew by sad experience.

As recently as 1920, more than a half-million Americans died from diphtheria, whooping cough, measles, syphilis, intestinal infections, kidney infections, tuberculosis, influenza, and pneumonia. Since the discovery of antibiotics, Americans almost never die of the first four diseases, annual deaths from the next three conditions are down more than 95 percent, and deaths from influenza and pneumonia are down more than 60 percent. Allowing for today's larger population, 1.2 million Americans a year would be dying of these diseases if doctors were still using the pharmacology of 1920.

A recent graduate of a community-college nursing program, an adeptly programmed personal computer, and a pharmacy clerk can do more for more patients today than the helpless physician of the past. And all the prescriptions written by all the doctors in the land consume only 7 percent of American expenditures on health care, and they generally work well.

But politicians in many countries seem to despise the drug industry. Some control prices by law; others set their single-payer health-care systems to drive hard bargains with the producers.

A natural result is that companies based in countries with rigorous price controls, such as France, Italy, and Japan, tend to concentrate on manufacturing local copies of internationally successful drugs. Breakthrough drugs disproportionately originate in countries that do not regulate prices of new drugs, such as the U.S., Germany, Britain, and the Netherlands. The profit motive drives research and innovation. Protecting inventors' monopolies on new drugs might actually be more effective in delivering new drugs at reasonable prices. Some of the high price for new drugs is reasonably related to the high cost of developing drugs and seeing them through the testing and approval systems of the U.S., Europe, and Japan. Some of the high price is reasonably related to the low probability of successfully passing through the system to bring a new drug to market. For every new drug approved, pharmaceutical companies research thousands of compounds and test hundreds. The failures cost money also, and the failures are paid for on the backs of a few successes. But some of the high price of new drugs is unreasonably related to the relatively short term of patent monopoly and the rather high probability that successful drugs will be exposed to "me-too" competitors that are slightly different chemically but nearly the same medically. Even in the U.S., laws respecting generic competition—drugs that are exactly the same chemically—are deliberately filled with potential loopholes enabling generic drug companies to bring their products to market without expensive testing. This legalized counterfeiting has made generic drugs in the U.S. into an industry worth hundreds of billions of dollars, born and raised by members of congress intent on driving down the price of new drugs for consumers. They talk about the capitalist benefits of competition, but capitalism needs property rights just as much as competition. Lengthening the patent term for newly discovered drugs might even bring down the price because companies that invent drugs would not need to recoup their investments in the short run.

Who Pays for Health Insurance?

With a little help from the beneficiaries and some help from payroll taxes on workers and employers, the federal government pays for Medicare, a health-insurance program for people over 65 and disabled people of any age—which is to say that income taxpayers and business taxpayers are paying for it, as they do all other general functions of the federal government. About 40 million people are covered under Medicare. Many consider it the most successful government program in American history, but this is a short-sighted view. In the longer term, the Medicare program is on track to consume all the revenues of all the current federal taxes, leaving nothing for any other government function. Or, what is somewhat more likely, taxes will double over the next 30 years to pay for Medicare. Or, most likely, taxes will go up substantially and Medicare will not pay for as many things. Medicare will refuse to pay the full cost of medical services, and the beneficiaries who can afford to pay more will be charged more.

Out of 250 million Americans who are not yet eligible for Medicare, more than 150 million have varying levels of coverage from medical insurance plans sponsored by their employers. About 13 million pay for their medical insurance themselves. About 41 million people with very low incomes and few assets are covered by Medicaid and a variety of small state and federal programs.

More than 47 million Americans are without health insurance. One reason is that the federal government has seen to it that everyone has two lines of defense against health-care emergencies. First, hospital emergency rooms are required to treat everyone who shows up, whether or not they have means to pay. Second, if a person receives care without paying for it, the Medicaid program is supposed to pay the health-care expenses of those Americans who are without other means. Usually, however, Medicaid pays only part of the real cost. Providers have to raise their fees to everyone else to offset their losses on Medicaid patients. If a person is caught with too many assets to qualify for Medicaid but too few resources to pay a hospital bill, the hospital pursues the patient, but eventually writes off the debt and raises future charges to those patients who do pay. Another reason so many are without insurance is that state and federal mandates have distorted the market for health insurance, adding so many coverage mandates as to make sensible, affordable policies unavailable.

A national consensus in favor of health-care reform seems to be growing—as long as it provides more health care for more people at lower costs. Unfortunately, the free lunch table is closed, and the magic wands are on back order.

Health-care reform is harder and more treacherous than most people imagine—especially advocates who would put on employers' backs a heavy play-or-pay tax system requiring businesses to provide health insurance or pay premiums for a government insurance plan. Play or pay isn't health insurance; it's a payroll tax. This is not what Wal-Mart and the car companies had in mind when they created a coalition to lobby for universal health insurance. They were trying to get health care off their budgets and on to someone else's.

Free Choice at a Price

A better alternative to national health insurance would be national competition in health insurance, in which insurance companies, health maintenance organizations (HMOs), hospitals, doctor groups, and any other organizations compete to offer health-care plans. These would include affordable plans insuring against health catastrophes with low premiums and high deductibles, expensive first-dollar-coverage plans, or any combination of premiums and services that might appeal to consumers. Government welfare agencies would buy insurance to cover their charity cases.

An efficient market in health insurance would redistribute the money that Americans spend on health care. Everyone should select his own health-insurance program, and health insurers should be free to compete for business by offering a range of plans and prices. People must confront real, unsubsidized prices to make appropriate choices.

Imagine hundreds of companies competing for business on the basis of price and service, as if they were selling homeowners' insurance or investments. To keep costs low, they could work with groups assembled by churches, social clubs, neighborhood organizations, credit unions, banks, professional group assemblers, and, yes, even employers.

Can everybody afford such a system? At least as well as they can now—and probably far better. For those who cannot afford it, government welfare departments could subsidize premiums directly or put cash in the hands of those capable of making their own choices.

The most useful example of this idea already works for millions of federal workers. The Federal Employee Health Benefits Program is a multiple-choice system in which the government, as employer, lets workers choose which plan they like and then pays for three-quarters of the cost. An open season on health plans occurs each fall. A couple hundred insurance plans and HMOs market their services to federal workers.

That the government operates one of the nation's most efficient and competitive health-insurance systems yet cannot extend the system to citizens who want and need coverage is a testament to the scale and complexity of the federal government. That politicians cannot reform health care by adopting the good system they themselves use is a testament to the block-headedness of politicians.

A rambunctious market drives the Federal Employee Health Benefits Program. Each year in November is open season, when all beneficiaries—roughly 10 million of them—can switch from one health-insurance program to another. It's a measure of their satisfaction that only about 5 percent actually change plans.

At least a dozen choices are available in every locality where the federal government has operatives, and nearly two dozen in the center of officialdom inside the Capital Beltway. On average, the government pays 75 percent of the cost of most plans, up to a limit of $3,800 for individuals and $8,600 for families. What the workers pay beyond that is their choice.

Price differences among the plans reflect different coverage. All plans include the level of hospital and medical insurance that Americans who work for big companies take for granted. They vary freely and charge widely different amounts on coverage of routine visits, pharmaceuticals, mental illness care, dental care, hospice and skilled nursing care, rehabilitative therapy, and medical equipment.

The insurance companies and HMOs campaign hard to win business. They advertise, hold rallies, and collaborate with unions and other institutions to win the trust of their prospective customers. Independent advisers offer federal workers detailed analyses of plans. Plans that charge too much lose members every open season, and some have actually gone out of business.

As for cost to the employer, the price for the Federal Employee Health Benefits Program as a whole has been rising at less than half the rate seen by private employers.

This federal plan is not universal. One of the low-cost family plans costs about $2,400 a year, and even that is burdensome to a federal office worker making $50,000 a year or less. About 100,000 eligible federal workers have declined coverage. To help them, the U.S. should shift responsibility for health-insurance premiums from employers to employees and give all people the same tax break now available only for employer-paid plans. Under the current system, wages paid in the guise of health-insurance premiums are tax-exempt to the employee and tax-deductible to the employer. From the worker's point of view, a health premium dollar can be up to twice as valuable as a wage dollar. (The same is usually true of other employee benefits, such as pensions and life insurance.) This buying power of the tax-exempt health dollar is one reason that health-care inflation outstrips other inflation in the economy.

Because only the employer can use pretax dollars to buy health insurance, coverage goes with the job in our current system. The result, of course, is the insecurity that reformers call a crisis. The driving force for health-care reform today isn't a generous impulse to help 47 million uninsured Americans; it's the fear that one may join them. If employees can choose between employer-provided health insurance and pretax cash to pay premiums to the health-insurance plan of their choice, or if people caught up in poverty receive a voucher with which to purchase health insurance, they will acquire real economic power. Even better, health-insurance companies will have to work for the beneficiary, not the beneficiary's boss.

The U.S. health-care problem has been created by the absence of competition and consumer choice. That's why the Federal Employee Health Benefits Program should become the model for the nation.

Still out on the fringes of health-care politics is another good idea, the medical savings account. This raises individual choice to a higher power and provides a capitalist solution relying on savings and investment. Although it's the single best idea in health-care policy since Blue Cross introduced group insurance, medical savings accounts became a dividing line between Democrats and loyal Republicans.

The idea is to cut the cost of health insurance for most people by letting them buy their insurance with a high annual deductible—$3,000 is commonly suggested. Then the insured people, their employers, or the government places $3,000 in a tax-sheltered medical savings account that becomes the property of each insured person. The account owners can pay medical expenses with a debit card linked to the Medical Savings account and the back-up insurance. At the end of the year, the account owner gets to keep anything left in the account. They can accumulate it in the Medical Savings account or pay taxes on it if they choose to spend it on other things.

This puts all the incentives in the right place, on the right people. Employees get to use the employer's money for health care, but they acquire a reason not to waste it by running to the doctor for every sniffle and sprain. Employees do for themselves what HMOs are supposed to do with regulations, gatekeepers, and restraints on physicians.

If we must have a policy and system for health care, rather than a market, medical savings accounts and high-deductible private health insurance should replace any other form of insurance that covers the first dollar of expense. The government systems of Medicare for the elderly and Medicaid for the poor also would work far better under such a system.

Summary

Democracies have every right to choose national health care, but the people should know the cost in taxes and lost economic growth before they choose. There are other choices that would be better than a single government provider or a single government insurer.

9

The Capitalist Approach to Retirement Security: It's an Individual's Duty First

U.S. Social Security was sold to the American public during the New Deal of the 1930s as a sort of annuity, like a private insurance scheme in which all participants pay, by taxes, in advance of the benefits they receive. To appeal to the human desire to get something for nothing, the obligation to pay the Social Security tax is split evenly between workers and their employers. Employers receive no benefit from paying the tax; however, they could have paid the money to the workers as salary. The government, by investing tax receipts in government bonds, makes the payments without burdening other taxpayers. In theory, participants get what they and their employers paid for.

Of course it is not voluntary, and no private alternatives are offered. People who might think they can provide better for themselves are not given the choice. Social Security was mandatory from the very beginning, although some workers were excluded from the system. Gradually it has been made mandatory for nearly all workers.

Unfortunately for the popular illusion that Social Security is a responsible insurance plan, it actually is set up to pay benefits that aren't related to the taxes paid. The lowest income workers receive more than they and their employers paid in plus the earnings on those payments. The highest-earning workers receive much less than they would have earned if their taxes had been invested with an insurance company in a private annuity contract. The excess goes to low-paid beneficiaries.

Since the program began, Americans have been told that they and their employers are paying into the system, and they will be entitled to take out their promised benefits. They have been told their money is in a trust fund invested in government bonds, the safest form of investment.

This is not true. That is how the program was set up in 1935, but in 1939 it was transformed into a "pay-as-you-go" system, in which current Social Security revenues pay current benefits. Only what's left over after benefits are paid is put into the trust fund. In 1939, very few people had paid into the system and were eligible to retire. Though the original tax rate was 2 percent of the first $3,000 of wages—half paid by employers and half by employees—plenty of money was available to pay generous benefits to the early retirees.

The first beneficiary was Ida Mae Fuller, a legal secretary from Ludlow, Vermont. She had worked and paid taxes for three years under Social Security. When she retired in January 1940, her first monthly check was $22.54, which was generous in the extreme, considering that she had paid only $22 in Social Security taxes, matched by $22 paid by her employer. She beat the system starting with her second check, and she lived to be 100 years old. During her retired lifetime, Congress kept raising benefits. Although it also raised the Social Security tax rates, that didn't matter to retirees like Ms. Fuller. Her last monthly check, in January 1975, was for $112.60. In her life she received $22,888.92 for the $44 of taxes paid by her and her employer.

We must note that $112.60 was not enough to live on comfortably in 1975, but it was a lot better than what she would have received from a deposit of $44 in a private insurance annuity—15 cents a month. Where did the rest of the money for Ms. Fuller come from? It came from the taxes paid by working Americans after she retired, and that's the system that Social Security has used ever since. Even the much-discussed Social Security surplus (the excess of current taxes over current benefits) held in the Social Security trust fund is a small surplus compared to the part of the system that's funded on a pay-as-you-go basis.

The conversion of the system to pay-as-you-go created winners and losers. Ida Mae Fuller was a winner, as are most Social Security beneficiaries who reached age 65 before 2005. They paid relatively low tax rates for much of their working lives to receive relatively generous benefits for most of their retirements. Younger people are paying higher taxes to pay for the benefits of the baby-boomer generation, and that tax bill is likely to rise, to keep pace with the benefit burden. Eventually, the system will have a cash-flow crisis likely to reduce the value of their benefits.

Social Security is a tax-supported charity program disguised as an underfunded pension plan. To give low-wage workers a pension that exceeds the economic value of the taxes paid by them and their employers, Social Security dramatically shortchanges higher-income workers.

This flaw has been disguised by the immaturity of the system. Far more taxpayers than beneficiaries existed in the beginning, and every time Congress decided to raise benefits for everybody, it also forced more workers into the system to increase tax receipts. When that game ended, Congress raised the tax rate in stages, to its present rate of 6.2 percent.

To keep the welfare scheme popular with the majority of Americans, most recipients of all income classes have received more benefits than the economic value of their taxes.

That game is over, too. Now that today's workers are old enough to add up what they have been paying in taxes (doubling the direct tax to include the employer's share) and subtract the present value of their projected future benefits, they can see what a lousy deal it is for them—12.4 percent wage tax now and at least a 20 percent lifetime wage tax in the future, levied on all the nation's workers to pay a taxable benefit that won't even pay back what they put in—never mind a decent rate of return.

The preservationist school of Social Security reform teaches that the program's social benefits are more important than the financial costs and more important than the truth.

One faction of a Social Security study commission that reported in 1997 reflected this view: "Social Security is not about to expire and does not require heroic measures. Rather, the situation with Social Security is like that of homeowners living in a sound house that they very much like and that needs only to have its mortgage refinanced. There is no need to tear the house down, remodel it, or trade it for a different house." (Dozens of reports of study commissions are available on line at www.ssa.gov/policy/, operated by the Social Security Administration. The Cato Institute, a free-market think tank, has an informative web site of its own at www.socialsecurity.org.)

The view that Social Security doesn't need "heroic measures" relies in part on what the Social Security Administration calls "intermediate" economic and demographic assumptions, which lie between "optimistic" and "pessimistic." Unfortunately for taxpayers and beneficiaries, even the pessimistic assumptions are probably not pessimistic enough. People are living longer, having fewer children, and earning less than the Social Security Administration projects. Since the last major reform in 1983, all estimates have been revised several times, generally in the direction of less solvency for Social Security.

And even if the intermediate assumptions turn out to be right on target, the government's financial problem does not start decades from now when the trust fund runs dry, but much sooner, when Social Security tax receipts run short of the cost of the program. At that point, in 2017 by current estimates, the government will have to start redeeming Treasury bonds from the trust fund to make up the short-fall of Social Security taxes.

Social Security's trust fund is entirely invested in Treasury bonds, so Social Security assets are U.S. Treasury liabilities. Making with-drawals from the trust fund requires either new taxation or selling a new flood of bonds to the public. The price in the first instance could be an economic depression, or it could be inflation of the national debt. Or we could do both and get both unpleasant outcomes.

When Social Security preservationists glibly declare that "mod-est" reforms are required to maintain the program, that turns out to mean a 30 percent increase in payroll taxes plus increased taxes on benefits.

If Social Security finances were a house, this would be the situa-tion: The roof is leaking now, the kids are coming back home to live off Mom and Dad, the neighborhood has deteriorated, property taxes are way up, interest rates are rising, and the only available mortgages at the bank are adjustable-rate loans at five points over prime. We already owe more on the property than it's really worth, and we also have budgeted to sell it at a big profit to finance our retirement.

The United States "solved" the Social Security crisis in 1983. A bipartisan commission chaired by Alan Greenspan made proposals to raise taxes, reduce future benefits, and disguise these actions. A bipartisan Congress balked, but the Democratic Speaker of the House Tip O'Neill and Republican President Ronald Reagan worked out the differences. They raised taxes less, reduced future benefits less, and disguised these actions more. But they succeeded in defus-ing the problem for a generation.

Checks might have been reduced in 1983 if O'Neill and Reagan had not made their deal, but now the Social Security tax more than covers all benefits for this year, next year, and all years projected out to 2017. The accumulated excess of tax receipts over benefits, plus interest, is expected to provide an adequate supplement to taxes out to 2041.

But that does not mean that everything is okay until 2041. It's our responsibility now to fix things for the future. Social Security is in a continuing long-term crisis: Taxes aren't growing as fast as benefits, which are propelled by increases in the aged population and by cost-of-living increases that outstrip inflation.

Also, revenues in excess of benefits have been invested in U.S. Treasury bonds, which is like borrowing from your savings account to put money in your checking account. When you write checks, you congratulate yourself for cleverly having your cake and eating it, too.

The Social Security surplus is a chimera. Although Treasury bonds exist documenting every dollar of the $2 trillion owed to the Social Security trust funds, the money was borrowed from the trust funds and spent on general government programs. To redeem the trust funds' bonds and pay benefits, the Treasury will have to borrow from the public, more and more every year. This replacement borrowing will have real economic consequences, although no one can know when or if the camel's back will break.

The state's camel might not break it's back under the straws of Social Security alone. Even though the number of beneficiaries will about double over the next 35 years, taxes could be raised to cover full benefits, including cost-of-living increases. All it would take is a 25 percent increase in the tax on workers and employers. How many politicians would vote for that?

It All Started with Bismarck

The original state retirement pension program was instituted by Chancellor Otto von Bismarck for Germany in 1889. The retirement age was 70. Adult life expectancy in those days was about 72. If work back then began, on average, at 16, that gave 54 working and tax-paying years to finance 2 years of retirement, a work-to-retirement ratio of 27:1. The state could easily afford it.

Now move to the present. Imagine yourself as a person who started work at age 22 and wants to retire at 62, expecting to live until age 82—pretty much in keeping with the current U.S. averages. How much of your income must you save during 40 working years to provide enough income for 20 nonworking retirement years?

Suppose we take 70 percent of the wages you earned in your last year of work as a reasonable retirement-income goal. Many financial planners say you can get by on that. In addition, suppose that labor productivity and wages grow at a reasonable 1.5 percent annual rate during your career. And assume that you can save in a tax-deferred investment account. We need to specify one more variable: The real, after-inflation rate of return on your savings. The long-run historical average of pretax, real yields on long-term U.S. Treasury bonds is about 3 percent. Going forward, a conservative portfolio of stocks and bonds might be expected to return 4 percent over inflation, on average. Now let's calculate what savings rate is needed to have enough at retirement to purchase a 20-year annuity, which would provide the target retirement income.

Bad news: The required savings rate is over 14 percent of pretax income. Every working year, you need to save more than 14 percent of your total pretax income and invest these savings at a compound real return of 4 percent to finance 20 nonworking retirement years at 70 percent of the final year's wages. Compare this 14 percent required savings rate to the current U.S. savings rate, which averaged about 1.5 percent during the past five years. (You might add the appreciation on your house, but the experience of 2006 and 2007 suggest that would not be wise.)

Even a 14 percent savings rate might be too low a savings rate to generate financial security. Even from 1950 to 1990, the average U.S. personal savings rate was an insufficient 7.7 percent. If we take this as defining a historical norm and make the extreme assumption that the savings were entirely devoted to retirement, in a scenario of 40 working years and 20 retirement years, the savings would generate a retirement income of about 38 percent of ending wages.

These required savings can include some part of Social Security taxes, although the return on those taxes varies substantially with income and the future politics of Social Security. The savings also can include other involuntary savings, such as pension-plan contributions made by an employer—if an employee has a pension plan and if the employer remains solvent. In any case, providing for 20 retirement years with savings from 40 working years requires an intense commitment to saving large chunks of pay.

Fortunately, the retirement ages of 62 or 65 are neither magic nor unalterable. If you are going to live another 20 years, you could work longer. But Americans generally are going in the opposite direction. They are choosing shorter careers and longer retirements, if they can afford it.

Corporate early-retirement programs, designed to save compensation expense today by putting increased costs into the pension plan tomorrow, notably move the fundamental work-to-retirement relationship in the wrong direction and make adequate pension finance that much harder to achieve. If we change our example to early retirement at 57, the work-to-retirement ratio drops to 1.4:1. The required savings for a 70 percent wage replacement will be saving 20 percent of pay.

If you do continue working, the ratio rises rather quickly. Say you started work at 22 and matched the Bismarck plan's retirement age of 70, then lived to 82. That's 48 years of work and 12 years of retirement; the ratio rises to 4:1. The required savings for the annuity with 70 percent wage replacement falls to 7 percent of pretax income.

You also can put the question the opposite way: If you are saving for retirement at a given rate, how many years should you plan on working to have sufficient money for your life expectancy when you retire? Assume again that your career-long investment returns beat inflation by 4 percent a year, on average. If your savings rate is 6 percent of your pretax income, you will need to work 50 years to retire for 10 years at the age of 72, with a work-to-retirement ratio of 5:1. Save less than that, and retirement will be financially less pleasant. If you can manage to save 10 percent, your requirement falls to 44 years working, with 16 years of retirement, beginning at age 66, a work-to-retirement ratio of 2.8:1. Remember, you need a savings rate of 14 percent to retire at 62 with an expected retirement of 20 years. If you could adjust your personal work-to-retirement ratio to 5:1 by delaying retirement, your Social Security tax alone would provide the target retirement income—if it were invested in a personal retirement account. This would leave your employer's Social Security tax to cover the disability, survivors, and other "safety net" aspects of Social Security.

These basic, sobering calculations explain why most Americans and their pension plans are hoping for high returns on their investments in stocks and real estate. They can't reach a long and comfortable retirement any other way, unless they want to face saving a lot more each year or working long past age 62.

At the same time, however, the national debt and the expenses of government are pushing the capitalist economy toward higher taxes, less private investment, more consumption, and slower productivity growth.

More Straws for an Aging Camel

There's more to the Social Security crisis than just the Social Security program. As the baby-boom generation ages, it will also start drawing on the Medicare program.

The annual reports of the Social Security and Medicare trustees tell us that the combined annual costs of Medicare, Social Security retirement, and Social Security disability programs amount to about

40 percent of total federal revenues and about 7 percent of gross domestic product (GDP). These costs are projected to double to 14 percent of GDP by 2040 and then to rise further to 17 percent of GDP in 2080.

Since World War II, the average size of total federal revenues as a percentage of GDP has been 18 percent and has never exceeded 21 percent. The anticipated growth in costs for Social Security and Medicare as they exist indicate that the total federal revenue share of GDP must increase to wholly unprecedented levels, assuming that the rest of the government's activities remain important to the citizens.

Another way to look at the funding problem: The United States of America has unfunded promises to retirees and disabled persons that have a present value of more than $39 trillion over the next 75 years. Present value here means that if we had the cash (we don't) and invested it in world stock and bond markets at current market rates (we won't), the earnings and principal plus pay-as-you-go taxation at current rates would be enough to pay the liabilities of Social Security and Medicare for 75 years. (But the problem would rise up again in the 76th year.)

Social Security is the simpler program, and its imbalances would be easier to resolve if we wanted to do so and had sufficient political capital. Actuaries estimate that, over the next 75 years, Social Security benefits will have a present value that exceeds the revenue due under current law by $6.5 trillion. This includes $1.9 trillion from the so-called Social Security trust fund because it is just an accounting device. It measures the cumulative Social Security revenues spent on other government programs during the current period in which revenue has exceeded expenses.

To redeem the bonds in the trust fund, the government will have to tax or borrow $1.9 trillion in the open market. It will need another $4.6 trillion of present value, from taxes or borrowing, to supplement revenues from the existing tax to pay all promised benefits after the trust fund runs out in 2040.

The more-or-less easy way to do this is to raise Social Security taxes today from 12.4 percent to 14.4 percent (half of it nominally paid by employers and the other half deducted from employee pay), as long as the extra revenues are invested in private markets, not Treasury bonds. Another more-or-less easy way is to cut everybody's benefits, current and future, by about 13 percent, again with the proviso that the savings be put in the global capital market and not shifted from one of Uncle Sam's pockets to another. A third way is to raise the retirement ages for a given benefit by about five years.

Higher taxes are not universally popular. Benefit cuts would turn members of AARP (the former American Association of Retired Persons) into angry radicals. And most Americans are eager to retire at 62, not 67 or 72. But the Social Security problem can be fixed this way, although we have given the job to shortsighted lawmakers who can't see beyond the next election. What's hard and maybe politically impossible about Social Security is the job President George W. Bush tried to begin in 2005: Turning it from a pay-as-you-go welfare program into an advance-funded, individual retirement-savings program.

In any case, Social Security benefits are driven only by demographics: More people are going on Social Security payrolls as the baby-boomer generation retires, and all people are living longer, getting older, and collecting more benefits. If medical science delivers on our optimistic speculation about much longer life spans, the whole idea of retirement will have to change. Social Security and pensions can't cover 85 years of retirement on savings from 45 years of work.

Medicare, however, is driven by demographics, plus the rising cost of medical care and the rising desire for more and more care to live longer. The result is a bigger problem: Whereas actuaries compute the 75-year deficit of the Social Security program at 1.3 percent of annual GDP, Medicare's hospital insurance deficit over the same period is 2.27 percent of annual GDP.

The Medicare hospital insurance trust fund surplus is much smaller than that of Social Security, and we are already drawing it down. Moreover, there's more to Medicare than the hospital insurance program, also known as Part A. Hospital Insurance at least is partly funded by a 2.9 percent payroll tax. At $200 billion in 2007, it paid for a little less than half the total program.

Supplementary medical insurance, or Part B, pays a large share of beneficiaries' bills for physician and outpatient services, and it cost about $175 billion in fiscal 2007. Part C is a private insurance alternative to Parts A and B. Part D is the new prescription-drug coverage, which cost more than $50 billion in fiscal 2007.

Beneficiaries pay 25 percent of the cost of Parts B, C, and D; the rest is automatically transferred from the general operating budget of the federal government.

Some might say Parts B, C, and D can never have a deficit because their spending is covered by the federal deficit. It's better to say they are a main cause of the federal deficit.

Add up 75 years of expenses for Medicare's Parts A, B, C, and D, and subtract all the different revenues that pay for them: the Medicare payroll tax, the premiums paid by beneficiaries, a tax on upper-income Social Security benefits, and an involuntary contribution from the state Medicaid programs. The result: dedicated revenues that gradually rise from under 2 percent of GDP today to about 3 percent in 2080. Meanwhile, expenses will rise not so gradually, from under 2 percent of GDP to around 11 percent.

Add up the whole operation—Social Security plus Medicare in all its parts—and you'll discover that we are in the first years of a growing funding disaster. Never mind the widely publicized and far-off dates when the trust funds go broke. They serve only to make us complacent. The first year that the Social Security tax surplus failed to cover the general revenues needed for Medicare was 2006. Here we are.

From here on, the social safety net unravels. Its actuarial claim on general revenues rises to nearly 3 percent of GDP by 2020, nearly 7 percent in 2040, more than 8 percent in 2060, and nearly 10 percent in 2080—over and above payroll taxes and other revenues.

If percentages of GDP are too abstract to understand, U.S. Comptroller General David Walker offered figures in cold, hard cash in a 2007 report from his Government Accountability Office: Using present value, which is the amount of money we would have to invest now at today's interest rates, adjusted for inflation, to have enough money to pay all benefits in the future, he reported the present value of the Social Security shortfall is about $6.5 trillion—a little more than today's national debt held by the U.S. public and foreign investors. The present value of the Medicare shortfall is about $30 trillion.

These numbers could turn out to be too small. Congress might expand either program, as it did recently by adding the Medicare prescription-drug benefit without funding the $8 trillion additional shortfall. Or a medical breakthrough might let everyone live longer and collect more benefits. The present value of the whole problem is already three times the nation's annual economic output and 15 times annual federal revenues.

This is a problem that even dynamic capitalism can't solve without hurting someone.

Slouching to the Future

The natural result of the Social Security–Medicare mess is a brewing political rebellion, still muffled for the time being but growing more potent with every year that passes without fundamental reform.

President George W. Bush thought the time was ripe for reform in 2005, but he was wrong. Sooner or later, probably later, today's working Americans are going to have to recognize that they paid for the first generations of Social Security retirees, rich and poor, but no crowd of younger people is going to pay so much in turn for their retirement.

Unless the system invests in private enterprise, and those investments continue to earn historically high returns, the back end of the baby-boomer generation—born in the 1950s and early 1960s—will pay for its own retirement. It can pay now with higher taxes, while most of its members are still employed, or pay later during retirement, with reduced benefits. If the boomers don't like it, that's tough. Most of those to whom they should complain, such as President Franklin D. Roosevelt and the members of Congress who made funding and benefit decisions in the 1960s and 1970s, are dead.

A democracy cannot easily handle any issue if successful resolution creates many economic losers and few winners. Just look at the strikers in 2006 and 2007 protesting changes in the government pension schemes in France and elsewhere in Europe. Those governments promised more than their economies could deliver, in part because their welfare taxes hamstring economic performance.

For their whole lives, baby boomers have been the 400-pound canaries of American society. The children born between 1946 and 1964 have been the birds who sit anywhere they want, whose whims rule the nation. When they were children, the country moved to the suburbs and forced municipalities to build thousands of new schools. The government built the interstate highway system, which let Mom and Dad take them on a new kind of vacation. When they were teenagers, the country went youth-crazy and idolized idealistic college students. The government provided a new system of college loans and subsidized the construction of college facilities. When they were young adults, the country changed its banking system to provide credit cards and mortgages so that they could go deeply into debt to have it all right then and there. The government changed the bank-ruptcy laws and eventually taxed everybody to bail out the thousands of lenders who accommodated profligate boomers.

When they reached middle age, Wall Street rebuilt itself to pro-vide mutual funds and brokerage accounts to help them pay off debts and build some wealth. The government created new tax-advantaged retirement accounts and enhanced the attractiveness of old ones.

What other generation has had its music playing on the radio for their whole lives? There were no big-band oldies stations when the boomers were kids, but every city now has two or three oldies stations playing the boomers' favorites.

No other generation enjoyed a 17-year bull market, marred only by one big recession and one little one. Their parents weathered three recessions during the Eisenhower administration alone. Sure, it's coincidence that microchip technology got started when the boomers were teens and it was just good luck for everybody that shrinking transistors made computing and communications ever more powerful, as if on a schedule. But it's not coincidence that the national economy struggled when the boomers were young and inex-perienced, and it then took off as the boomers hit their productive stride.

Boomers are frequently condemned, even by their own pundits, as spoiled, self-absorbed, and greedy. Some say they were nursed on demand feeding according to the theories of Dr. Spock, and they never got over it. But with all their annoying flaws, boomers in their vast numbers are the best thing that ever happened to the American economy. The demand of 77 million credit card–wielding consumers, many of them well educated to demand the best, has driven produc-ers all over the world to do their best on price and performance. And the engineers, scientists, doctors, and managers turned out by those expanded schools and colleges have provided the means to design and supply better products and services valued around the world.

That's a trend that should continue for as much as two more decades. But it's equally true that boomers will impose at least one more major shift on the American economy, and this one not for the better. As they retire, boomers will convert themselves from producers to pure consumers. A huge percentage of U.S. cash flow will be devoted to paying their Social Security and their Medicare.

How this will be done has never been clear. Without changes in the programs, Social Security and Medicare will shoulder aside most other nondefense government spending by the 2030s or impose huge tax increases on younger generations of working people.

But it has always seemed clear that this would be done, somehow. The boomers are too numerous to mess with, and they have always gotten their way.

We have also heard that boomers pose another financial threat, to themselves and other investors. Private retirement savings, though for the most part fully funded, are funded in securities markets, and some analysts have warned that as boomers tap pensions and investments to finance consumption in retirement, they will drain capital from the markets and cause a Wall Street crash in 2020, or thereabouts.

It seems logical, even just, and certainly a bit ironic. If boomers' saving and investing have driven the market up tenfold from the base of 1982, and even if that goes on smoothly for many more years, won't boomers' spending down their investments ultimately tank the market?

No.

Sure, markets will fluctuate. Corrections and probably one or two meltdowns will occur before we get to 2020, and probably more thereafter. And the U.S. government has so much power to affect markets and the economy that it's always possible that some future statesman will lead us into another Great Depression. But the flow and ebb of boomer capital will not cause the crash of 2020 or any other year.

This tide will move very slowly. Even the most speculative boomers will become more cautious as they approach retirement age. They will gradually shift their new investments toward bonds and stocks that pay dividends. In retirement, they will consume dividends and coupon payments rather than reinvest them, but this will not change the flow of funds into the market much. Accommodating this trend, companies themselves will also become more cautious as they age. A company that was a successful speculation in the nineties reached comfortable prosperity in the aughts and gradually will reflect that prosperity in dividends paid in the teens.

The key word is gradually. No boomers with sense or a financial adviser will cash in all their growth stocks on their 65th birthday. The typical boomers will sell securities only as needed, mindful of the tax consequences. The capital-gains tax will hike the price of disinvestment, and the regular income tax will take a major bite out of funds withdrawn from individual retirement accounts (IRAs), 401(k) plans, and other tax-deferred retirement vehicles.

Even if demography is destiny, and even if boomers want to sell in a mad rush, buyers will exist—foreign buyers, putting newly earned wealth to work in the safest markets in the world. As long as the U.S. government does not do anything to spoil the national economic reputation, boomers in millions will be able to sell to foreign investors in even greater millions.

Perhaps more interesting to American trend-spotters, lots of American investors will be buying, too. The overlooked demographic feature of twenty-first-century America is this: The baby boomers recently ceased to be the most numerous generation in U.S. history.

Make Way for X and Y

The aging of America has been a widely expected trend, but the twenty-first century may not be ruled by graying boomers after all. The boomers must make way for Generations X and Y, otherwise known as the birth dearth and the baby rebound.

Generation X followed the baby boom, and its spokespeople were feeling lost and unloved in the early nineties when they named the generation. We don't know what Y stands for—neither do they as yet—we just know it follows X.

Boomers had fewer children, but they also delayed having families, so lots of their kids missed Generation X and are concentrated in the cohorts born after 1980. Joining them in Generation Y are the children of immigrants who came in the large waves of migrants— legal and illegal—arriving here since 1975.

The result is that there are roughly 77 million boomers, born between 1947 and 1964; 60 million Gen Xers, born between 1965 and 1980; and 80 million members of Generation Y, born between 1980 and 1995. (The next generation is still too young to have its own nickname. Generation Z is obvious but not foreordained.)

If demographics is destiny, then the United States could have a different destiny from the one we have expected. Perhaps the baby boomers will not be permitted to tax Generations X and Y into poverty or bind the government to the bidding of AARP and its allied groups of lobbyists for greedy geezers.

The less-numerous postbaby-boom generations will inherit financial rubble if the Social Security and Medicare systems fall apart on schedule, sometime between 2030 and 2060. But at least the better-off people of the older generation could do something remarkably practical to help their younger relations get ready for the Social Security crisis.

Current law allows parents and grandparents to make tax-free gifts of up to $10,000 a year to children. As soon as the kids start earning money, they can open tax-deferred IRAs. Oldsters can give the youngsters money—$2,000 a year, let's say, to leave room for the kids to put some of their own money in—to fund the IRAs. The kids can't pull the money out without a tax penalty. The reason early investment is so important is that money invested at 10 percent doubles every 7.5 years if it isn't taxed. So the earlier somebody starts a tax-deferred retirement savings plan, the more doublings will take place.

If your grandchild started retirement saving at age 20, the $2,000 put away in the first year would become $256,000 at age 70 if it earns an average 10 percent a year (a generous return, no doubt). But $2,000 put away by scrimping at age 27 would become only $128,000 at age 70. And $2,000 put away at age 62 would be only $4,000 at age 70.

Almost nobody is wise enough and prudent enough to start saving for retirement out of earnings from a paper route or an after-school job. Wisdom and prudence come with long experience. The IRA gift is a way for older people to share their wisdom and prudence with the young before it's too late.

The federal government could make it easier by allowing IRA contributions for any living person, regardless of age or income. Another 20 years of deposits and another 20 years of compounding would make retirement savings that much more powerful. If the government also made a donation itself on behalf of each of its youngest citizens, IRAs could go much farther in replacing the unsteady Social Security system.

Social Security could be converted to something that works more like a private retirement plan. Genuine reform would reduce guaranteed benefits and make up the difference with a forced savings plan, in which participants would keep ownership and investment control of their retirement accounts. The government would select and regulate a variety of investment vehicles; the participants would allocate their assets among them.

Unfortunately, the current system was created and is defended by those who stress the "social" aspect and ignore financial security. They believe in making everyone secure without reference to their effort or savings. They reject the idea of giving participants power to make investment choices, fearing that too many would make bad choices.

A capitalist Social Security system should place its assets in private markets. Even if stocks don't continue to produce greater returns than Treasuries, Social Security funds won't be used merely to finance the government deficit.

But many Americans see danger in individual ownership of retirement assets. Some are simply afraid of the stock market and the bond market, where invisible and impersonal economic forces rule. Others fear political pressure to open tax-sheltered retirement savings to other, more immediate uses, such as down payments on homes, college tuition bills, medical expenses, or covering expenses during a period of unemployment. In other words, they fear people making their own choices about what to do with their own money. That's nothing to fear—it's something to welcome.

Summary

Saving for retirement is no more sacred than saving for any other purpose. Savings is money, and money is fungible, which means that if you don't use it here, you can use it there: People with hefty retirement accounts do not fear putting a medical bill on a credit card or college tuition on a second mortgage. Lenders look at their entire net worth and won't turn away business just because much of their wealth is retirement savings.

The key is making savings a foundation of society by making it an individual responsibility.

10

A Capitalist Look at the Current Economy

At the beginning of 2008, Americans began to perceive that the United States was slipping into a recession. Energy prices had touched $100 a barrel, and the high cost of fuel was working through the economy like a tax, raising prices and suppressing demand for almost everything. The biggest problem, however, wasn't fuel costs but the disruption caused by the bursting of a bubble in housing. Home construction is one of the largest industries in the U.S., but it had grown too fast.

Ever since the Great Depression, when specialized housing finance with federal government backing made home buying less risky and more rewarding, housing has been riding a great wave of federal sponsorship and federal subsidy.

American homeowners enjoy many benefits, the biggest of which are income-tax deductions for mortgage interest paid and for real estate taxes paid. Capital gains taxes, which are paid on most types of investment profits, are waived on the first $500,000 of profits on home investments. The government also has created financial institutions to back housing loans and provide incentives for investors to lend to the housing industry.

These subsidies and structures reduce the cost of mortgage and tax payments, but the value of these subsidies is dubious. Prices of houses have risen to offset the advantage of the subsidies. Every financial innovation in housing has driven up the price of houses, and of course, the long flood tide of rising prices made more and more people eager to own their own homes. Because high prices have made houses harder to afford, however, those eager buyers have borrowed more to get their starts and added to the leverage that makes housing capital the most powerful economic force in America.

The value of U.S. residential property, just under $21 trillion on September 30, 2007, far exceeded the stock-market worth of all public companies. Nearly 70 percent of American housing units are owned by the occupants. Most of their wealth is tied up in the appreciated price of houses they bought years ago.

Unfortunately, trees do not grow to the sky. The success of housing as an investment carried with it the seeds of failure. In the hottest areas of appreciating house prices—such as Florida, California, and Arizona—home prices grew much faster than people's ability to pay for them.

Borrowing more, on easy credit terms, was the solution for a few years, especially between 2003 and 2006. Lenders offered loans with low down payments or no down payments. They even offered negative down payments—lending more than a property was worth. A great many loans issued in the bubble years were also adjustable-rate mortgages with lower-than-market "teaser" rates to start. Some borrowers signed up knowing only dimly that they would be required to pay higher rates within a few years. By 2007, many were losing a gamble they might not have known they were making: that their houses would appreciate or that loans would be cheaper before the rate reset. As 2008 opened, 1.5 million homeowners faced increases in monthly payments of 30 percent or more on houses they could barely afford at the teaser rates.

Fueled by easy credit, some buyers were simply speculators, using borrowed money to buy homes they did not intend to occupy. Before the bubble burst, a common get-rich-quick strategy was to pay a small down payment on a condominium in a building under construction, then "flip" it—sell it for a profit when the building was finished and ready for occupancy. They expected that, if prices were going up, they would be able to sell later at higher prices.

This is sometimes called the "greater fool theory," meaning speculators may know they are paying foolish prices for assets but do it anyway because greater fools are coming along behind to buy and provide them with their profits. Low interest rates extended the boom time, but debt alone could not create enough greater fools to make high prices stick permanently. Eventually, the inflated market ran out of buyers.

Everyone in the real-estate bubble forgot to look at real-estate history: House prices go up and down. Sometimes they languish for years. Timing a real-estate cycle is dangerous. Lucky bets may pay off in the short term, but the game is like musical chairs: Eventually some owners are stuck with houses they can't afford to keep and can't sell, except at a loss. In the real-estate crunch that started in 2007, it looked as though there would be a couple million owners in that situation.

The safe and responsible way to play real estate is to save a 20 percent down payment. This gives the purchaser some room to make a short-term mistake. Making a 1 percent down payment means you can afford more house, but it also means you can lose your entire investment if the house price drops 1 percent. If the price drops farther, you owe more than your property is worth. The small down payment also creates a larger mortgage with a higher monthly payment, one you may not be able to afford in hard times.

Time is on the side of investors taking this approach, just as time is on the side of stock-market investors who discipline themselves to invest every month in a portfolio of mutual funds. In the long run, home prices generally rise at least as fast as currency depreciates. Population growth adds a bullish bias that usually pushes house prices ahead a little faster than inflation.

If this sort of investing sounds antediluvian, remember that every now and then a flood of bad debt can bring lower prices. It came to California in the early 1990s; it came in Colorado, Texas, and Boston in the 1980s. Those who couldn't wait out the downswing sold at substantial losses. Some distressed borrowers just moved away and mailed their house keys to the bank. Banks that had financed overpriced houses became owners. They sold foreclosed and abandoned houses for whatever they could get, even if it was for less than the amounts of the loans they had made. The losses offset the profits they had made on the way up and the low prices held back the housing market for years.

Rogues' Gallery

The twenty-first century real-estate bubble was produced with easy money, and it came to an end with a credit crunch. But the disaster was made by human errors. Some famous, supposedly responsible people should have taken the blame along with thousands of obscure but important financiers and millions of impecunious borrowers.

Candidates for blame should include

- **Alan Greenspan**—The "maestro" of the Federal Reserve pounded the monetary gas to get the country out of recession in 2001. Interest rates were far below normal, and the Fed kept supplying more credit anyway.

- **President George W. Bush**—The "compassionate conservative" pushed tax cuts and allowed the Republicans in Congress to boost spending as if they were old-time Democrats. He also perpetuated polices inherited from his predecessor.

- **President Bill Clinton and his housing promoters at the Department of Housing and Urban Affairs, Henry Cisneros and Andrew Cuomo**—With legislation and regulation, they made borrowing and lending ever easier during the 1990s. They helped get the housing boom started.

- **William R. Fair and Earl J. Isaac**—They started Fair Isaac, a credit analysis company that provides credit scores based on objective criteria. Fair Isaac analytics are used in three out of four U.S. mortgage originations, and the company sells 10 billion credit scores a year. The company's objective analytics turned credit decision-making from a character judgment into a commodity. One could package hundreds of individual loans with the same credit score as if they were all the same.

- **Wall Street investment bankers**—Bankers packaged thousands of individuals' mortgages into "collateralized mortgage obligations" (CMOs). There was supposed to be safety in numbers. The investment bankers created a greater illusion of safety by slicing the CMOs into parts graded by risk, measured by credit scores. Investors in the highest-rated slices weren't supposed to lose money unless a large percentage of the mortgages defaulted. Investors and speculators who bought lower-rated slices had fewer assurances but were promised higher returns on their investments. This process of securitization started out reducing risk but gradually increased it. The true quality of the mortgages in the CMOs and similar securities could be very different from their average credit scores but very hard for investors to measure on their own. Most investors, indeed, did not perform independent analyses. As time went on, the bankers slipped more and more risky mortgages into the packages, and those risky mortgages supported borrowers as they paid higher and higher prices for houses.

- **Rating agencies**—These agencies, particularly Standard & Poor's and Moody's, swallowed the financial alchemy that supported CMOs. They were willing to believe that portfolio construction could trump high leverage and poor quality in a package of loans. They never imagined that millions of loans could all go bad in a short time, even though millions of loans were being written with adjustable rates that could require much higher payments in a few years. If the rating agencies did not succumb to an alchemical elixir, perhaps it was money. Issuers, not investors, pay the rating agencies to analyze and rate their securities.

- **Supposedly professional investors**—Chasing yield, they rushed to put their funds' money into highly rated securities they did not understand because they did not analyze them independently. They should have realized if high-risk slices of CMOs were paying investors a small premium over the yield from really secure investments such as U.S. Treasury notes there were likely to be problems in the future. This was a sign from the market that buyers were ignoring risk and that a bubble was forming.

- **Predatory lenders, crooked appraisers, and brokers**—Their chief concern was to receive fees paid up front at the signing of a mortgage. The worst of these made their living inducing old folks with free-and-clear homes to become speculators in real estate and credit. Predatory lenders wrote mortgages just to collect inflated fees, knowing that they could sell the mortgages in the secondary market and let other investors deal with the problems that would surface later. Loans that seemed too good to be true often were. A typical example from a mail-order loan leaflet says, "Start saving now with our 1.750 percent loan program. It's almost impossible not to qualify! And it's fast and easy. Borrow up to 100 percent of the value of your home and take cash out for any purpose. Use the cash for anything you want. Pay off high-interest debt or tax liens, take a vacation or finance your child's education. It's up to you." According to the fine print, the loan would reset to 7 percent in one year, more than tripling the monthly payment.

- **Predatory borrowers**—A great many of the weakest loans were given to people who would not have qualified for them if they had told the truth about their incomes, their assets, and their credit histories. As many as 70 percent of mortgages that defaulted in the first year turned out to have false information on the original loan applications. BasePoint Analytics, a banking security consultant, reviewed a sample of 16,000 mortgages drawn from mortgages written between 1997 and 2006, including about half written in 2005 and 2006. Applications with false information were five times as likely to go into default in the first six months of the life of the loan.

> There were lies about income, lies about the value of houses, lies about employment, lies about credit history, and lies about the borrower's intention to live in the houses. Credit scoring provided no security when scores were based on lies. Eager lenders must share the blame because they did not check the facts, but predatory borrowing was at least as big a factor in the bubble as predatory lending.

Henry Kaufman, who acquired the nickname "Dr. Doom" for his prescient pessimism during financial crises in the 1970s and 1980s, has noted that financiers have redefined liquidity over the past couple of decades. Liquidity used to mean cash, or assets that certainly could be converted to cash with the stroke of a pen.

"Firms and households today often blur the distinction between liquidity and credit availability," Kaufman said in a speech in March 2007, just before housing troubles became widely apparent.

"When thinking about liquid assets, present and future, it is now commonplace to think in terms of access to liabilities," Kaufman said. He meant that Americans had come to think of wealth as something they can borrow, not something that they own. In modern America, a person with a $50,000 bank line of credit behaves with the same confidence as a person with $50,000 in a savings account.

If personal liquidity is redefined as what you can borrow with the stroke of a pen, then individuals can add up all the limits on the credit cards in their wallets, the permissible overdraft on their checking accounts, margin-loan limits on their brokerage accounts, and home-equity loan checks in their desks. Maxing them out, they may command two years' salary, or more if they had worked at expanding their credit when lenders were feeling frisky.

Such models of modernity should stop to calculate the monthly minimum payment required to make payments on all that borrowing. How many months could they go before their personal house of cards collapses? For many Americans, the answer is quite daunting: maybe

two or three months, maybe one year, maybe two weeks if there's a
job loss in the family.

Corporate liquidity in modern America is not much different.
Companies maintain credit lines that would have constituted the
mark of Cain many years ago, confident that they can borrow their
way through any crisis.

When people or corporate treasurers write checks on air to
achieve liquidity, they should think of Owen Glendower, the Welsh
magician who tries to impress Henry Hotspur in an early scene of
Shakespeare's Henry IV, Part I. Glendower brags that he can "call
spirits from the vasty deep!" Hotspur gives him no credit: "Why, so
can I; or so can any man. But will they come?"

What shook the markets in 2007 and 2008 was a refusal of the
spirit of easy money to come from the vasty deep. America was
undergoing an agonizing reappraisal of the power and security of
credit.

Politicians of both parties offered remarkably similar ideas about
how to fix the mortgage meltdown. They would perform "voluntary"
reconstructions of the terms of some mortgages, especially the
adjustable-rate mortgages that require higher monthly payments
when interest rates rise. They proposed giving some borrowers a
chance to continue their gambles by freezing the adjustment for a
year or two or five. Maybe house prices will go up; maybe rates will
come down; maybe there will be a miracle.

All sides agreed that the credit economy ran out of greater fools,
at least temporarily. A credit-stretching process that started in the
1980s finally ran its course. But Americans should not try to fix the
mortgage mess and the credit crunch with lower interest rates, bigger
subsidies, and easier money. Unrealistic loans should be terminated.
No serious difference exists between renting and paying on a no-
down payment mortgage. The sooner lenders foreclose, the sooner

the lenders can book the losses and borrowers can go back to renting, all on newly realistic terms.

The cure for excessive leverage is financial failure. The sight of banks and mutual funds suffering losses will encourage others to tighten their standards and be more vigilant.

Capitalism requires risk to justify the returns that create more capital. Without risk there will be no capital.

Booms and Busts Born in Debt

Manias and bubbles such as the twenty-first century housing bubble seem to afflict capitalist societies about once a generation. Three early ones are among the most famous, and they were dealt with in ways that should help us understand how to deal with ours.

A fervent speculation in tulip bulbs disrupted the Netherlands in 1636 and 1637. Tulips were much loved and admired, and it was a mark of distinction to display the newest and most exotic varieties painstakingly raised from seed. These were always scarce at first because duplication depended on bulb-splitting, and that process had to start with one bulb, then two, four, eight, and so on, doubling each generation until they would eventually become quite common and not expensive.

The Dutch were already trading commodities such as grain and coffee, they were already trading contracts for future delivery of those commodities, and they were already borrowing money to make their deals on their exchanges. Sometimes this entailed considerable risk—a crop might fail; a shipload of coffee might be lost at sea. The Dutch were among the first Europeans to make sophisticated judgments about risk that affected prices in the markets.

The risks of the tulip business were actually quite easy to control because predicting how long it would take a particular tulip cultivar to become common was easy. So trading tulip bulbs and especially contracts for the future delivery of tulip bulbs was a natural addition to the existing Dutch markets. It was so natural that many people entered the business of trading tulip futures, and their enthusiasm drove prices higher, which brought more people into the business of growing tulips, creating new cultivars on which to base new futures contracts, and so on. At a time when a family could live on 150 florins a year, a single rare and highly prized bulb could sell for 1,000 florins. At the height of the tulip mania, the record price was 6,000 florins for one special bulb. But not for long: Records indicate that prices of tulip bulb futures rose by a factor of 20 in three months, peaking in February 1637. Three months later they were back where they had been.

A rational basis existed for the high prices and for the low prices that followed: Ownership of a bulb that produced a marvelous flower could pay dividends on schedule over a long period of time—if the flower remained popular, if the plant did not mutate, if enough buyers of bulbs were always available. But fashions change, the plants change, and speculative buyers only buy while prices are rising.

Sooner or later, prices top out. The object for sale eventually goes to the highest bidder in the crowd. In an auction, the buyer cannot turn around and sell it to anyone in that crowd for more money. In the tulip bubble, the market took three months to find that last bidder. When he was found, prices began to fall—a process not much different from the collapse of the U.S. stock market bubbles in 1929 and 2000, or the collapse of the U.S. housing bubble in 2007.

Another aspect of the tulip mania that has a contemporary parallel to the U.S. housing crisis was that the government intervened to help some favored constituents. In February 1637, the distributors of tulip flowers were harmed by the high prices of flowers dictated by the high prices of bulbs. The Dutch florists' guild convinced the Dutch parliament to declare that all futures contracts were optional. Putative buyers need not buy the bulbs. They could get out of their deals by paying a small fee to the putative sellers. This ruined the bulb market almost instantly. Some speculators, however, had seen the change coming—they apparently included leading mayors and members of Parliament. These well-informed traders were able to sell out before the crash.

Depression and Recovery

The best-remembered speculative collapse in America is the Great Depression of the 1930s. The American boom of the 1920s was not unusually vibrant or excessive, but it came to a worse end than most booms, in a worldwide depression.

"Depression" is a word that evolved in economic history. Once it was a euphemism. People spoke of depressions when they wanted to avoid the use of the word panic. The worldwide Great Depression spoiled that forever. Now we talk of recessions when we want to avoid facing the word depression.

Just as small innovations in credit can inflate a bubble, so small mistakes can start an economic snowball rolling downhill. The stock-market crash of 1929 need not have been a very important event, but monetary mismanagement and protectionism that followed the crash put millions out of work in a decade-long Great Depression.

The Depression did more than just put people out of work. It frightened people out of their wits. People should have understood that a market crash was a likely response to such events as an American stock-market bubble in the 1920s and the changes of power and wealth after World War I. In the early 1930s, better, faster communication by cable and radio made people realize that bad times were happening around the world, and they leaped to the conclusion that no relief was in sight. Their fear strengthened a normal popular fear of foreign competition that raised tariffs around the world, and the suppression of trade helped make the Great Depression great.

The great English economist John Maynard Keynes had analyzed the problems of economic adjustment after World War I. He had warned that Britain and France could not extract sufficient reparations from Germany to repay the cost of the war for the victors. Even if Germany were forced to pay everything, the one-sided terms of trade would actually harm Britain and France, Keynes said. He was right: Germany, Britain, and France bungled their monetary policy and set off a worldwide boom from 1924 to 1929. Unwinding that boom helped set the world on the road to depression.

When the Depression arrived, however, Keynes treated it as a shortage of money that could be cured with a good, stiff dose of inflation. He counseled the nations of the world to abandon the gold standard, drive down the value of their paper currency by printing more of it, and fool people into believing that if they held more dollars or francs or pounds they were richer, better off, and able to spend without risk, even in the obviously dangerous times in which American unemployment reached 25 percent. Most nations, from Hitler's Germany to Franklin D. Roosevelt's America, followed his advice. They tried to inflate, or reflate, or prime the pump, with government spending of newly created money.

Keynes saw that market prices and wages would not always fall to a level that would prompt consumers to buy and employers to start hiring. Businesses already suffering losses would have no interest in borrowing peoples' savings to invest in business expansion. They also would lay off workers, reducing total income, again increasing the supply of unsold goods, and so on in a downward spiral. A healthy economy needed another source of funding for consumption, beyond the total income of the people. That source was the governmental creation of money through deficit spending and inflation.

Just as the downward spiral seemed powerful, so too was the promise of an upward spiral that could be generated by governmental creation of money. If a government spends a million dollars on a new road, paying workers, contractors, concrete suppliers, and so on, who turn around and spend whatever they do not save, whatever they spend goes into the hands of other workers and suppliers who also spend and save, and so on. The original injection of easy money is multiplied each time the money changes hands. Keynes's math showed that the less people save, the harder money works. Keynes's advice works out to this: Saving bad. Spending good. If the private sector doesn't spend enough, the government should create more money and spend it. Deficit spending seemed to be the cure for economic downturns. Eventually, his advice worked, but only at the volume of deficit spending that came with World War II, not to cure the Depression but to win the war. World War II employed tens of millions of people and removed all previous political constraint on the size and power of the government.

Economically, World War II never ended. Governments never returned to balanced budgets, except briefly and usually by accident. Governments in Europe used deficit spending to rebuild and then to expand social services for protection against the return of the misery of the Depression. Since World War II, the effect of continual deficits has devalued the dollar and European currencies by more than 95 percent.

Keynes made many famous remarks, none more appropriate than the observation that "Practical men, who believe themselves to be quite exempt from any intellectual influence, are usually the slaves of some defunct economist. Madmen in authority, who hear voices in the air, are distilling their frenzy from some academic scribbler of a few years back." Keynes died in 1946. By the 1970s, Keynes had become that defunct economist. Each president after Roosevelt brought U.S. economic policy closer to the Keynesian ideal of using deficit spending to abolish slumps. Harry S. Truman's administration talked against inflation but lived with it. Dwight D. Eisenhower fought recessions with large spending programs such as the interstate highway system and the modernization of the Air Force, and his administration ran debts that seemed large at the time. John F.

Kennedy's economists invented an investment tax credit to stimulate business spending and proposed personal income-tax cuts that were enacted after his assassination. Lyndon B. Johnson's Great Society programs were aimed at relieving poverty, but an underlying satisfaction with the spending came from the grounds that it would keep the economy booming.

"We are all Keynesians now," said Richard M. Nixon said in 1971, dismissing criticism of his program for economic stimulus. By this he meant that nearly all capitalist countries and their politicians now accepted that economies would not reach full employment on their own, without government stimuli such as a tax cut or a spending increase funded by deficit spending. But inflation, the worst feature of the Keynesian strategy, dominated the 1970s. Three presidents— Nixon, Ford, and Carter—fought recessions with inflation and heavy-handed regulation. Each period of inflation (1970, 1974, and 1979) was followed by a worse recession; each recession (1971, 1975, and 1980) was followed by worse inflation.

By the late 1970s, many consumers of economic theories were fed up with Keynesian inflation and ready to accept Milton Friedman's warning that "Inflation is always and everywhere a monetary phenomenon." Friedman, an iconoclastic American who was the most influential capitalist economist of the post–World War II generation, meant that if Treasuries and central banks create too much money it drives up the price of goods and services.

Keynesians believed that loose monetary policies lower interest rates, which stimulates investment and hence employment, which, in turn, gives rise to multiple rounds of increased spending and increased real income as the initial stimulus worked its way through the economy. Friedman and a band of other monetarist economists held that money creation in excess of the growth rate of the economy would lead to inflation, and that lenders would demand higher interest rates to compensate for the loss of real value in the money by the time loans were paid off. The initial stimulus would wear out quickly, but the inflation would work its way through the economy, eventually offsetting the stimulus with the depressive force of higher interest rates.

Late in the administration of President Jimmy Carter, the Federal Reserve came under the sway of Friedman's monetarism. From 1979 through 1983, the Fed abandoned its attempts to control interest rates and sharply reduced the growth in the money supply. This experiment, carried forward to the early days of the Reagan administration, helped bring on the worst U.S. recession since the Great Depression, but it also choked off inflation and set the stage for two decades of almost continuous economic growth and low inflation. Policies set in motion by Paul Volcker, who was Carter's appointee as Federal Reserve chairman, were carried forward by Reagan's appointee Alan Greenspan. Neither Fed chairman was a dogmatic monetarist, but they both realized better than their predecessors that they had control of a dangerously powerful economic tool. They used it carefully, without speaking too clearly about what they were doing.

In the 1990s, however, Greenspan tried to do too much and too little at the same time. He seems to have regarded himself as the "maestro" of the economy (to use the title of a book about those years written by Bob Woodward). Under his leadership, the Federal Reserve tried to abolish the business cycle with doses of monetary discipline and indulgence. As early as 1996, the stock market was entering a period of "irrational exuberance," which was Greenspan's own term for the boom, but the Federal Reserve withdrew from its responsibility to regulate banking practices. Technology stocks soared. Then, the twentieth century ended with an apprehension that there would be a general computer meltdown—the "Y2K" problem. The Federal Reserve wanted to accommodate the investment in new computers and software to forestall this impending crisis, but it did not want that accommodation to be permanent. The Fed rapidly shifted back and forth between easy credit and tight money, trying to be the cure for all problems. When the 1990s bubble was followed by a bust, a recession began. The recession seemed to accelerate when the attacks of September 11th created general apprehension and uncertainty, and the Fed strode in with easy credit to make conditions better. This swing to easy money succeeded too well, touching off the real-estate bubble of 2003 to 2006.

Summary

One of the favorite phrases among financiers is "It's different this time." It always seems different because bubbles expand and pop in different ways. But the business cycle of expansion and contraction endures.

Keynes seems to have believed that people are basically irrational, at least in the mass of society. He considered economic prosperity to be the result of unfounded optimism, whereas depressions were caused by foolish pessimism. Monetarists like Friedman generally believe in "rational expectations"—that people act in the economy according to their perceptions of real opportunities or problems.

Those who accept the idea that economic cycles are irrational may come to believe with Keynes in a sort of economic royalism: A few well-informed policymakers must take command of the economy and manipulate it to benefit the rest of humanity. Observing that prices and wages don't drop in recessions quickly enough to clear markets of gluts (and that misery would result even if they did), Keynesians concluded that governments must stimulate demand.

The stock market bubble of the 1990s and the housing bubble of 2002-2006 had their origins in Keynesian stimulus. Economic booms and busts always have their causes in wrongheaded policies imposed by central bankers and governments trying to control economic forces that are actually too strong for them.

11

The Capitalist Quest for Productivity

The endless struggle to improve productivity at the heart of capitalism is not always welcome. Productivity can mean doing more with the same amount of effort, but a business trying to improve its productivity may have to reduce labor hours without reducing output. That means job losses, which are never popular. If productivity increases without actual job losses, it still may be a sign that the boss has found a way to make workers work harder. Speeding up an assembly line or forcing workers to adopt the recommendations of efficiency experts are unpopular with workers. After such experiences, any talk of productivity increases may be seen as a threat.

Recall from the introduction the painters whose skill with a brush was replaced by the mechanized perfection of the spray-painting machine. Suppose the boss had laid off the painters and replaced them with new workers, who were paid less and trained on the job to use the new equipment. After a brief drop in productivity while the new workers learned the skill of paint spraying, the business might well be more profitable, more productive, and be paying its workers less than before. Eventually, however, the business will need more workers. To attract more workers it will have to raise wages again.

We can understand the painters' fearing the investment in paint-sprayers, just as English hand weavers of the early nineteenth century feared the introduction of power looms so much that they rioted and destroyed the new machines. They were known as Luddites because they claimed their leader was "General Ned Ludd," a fictitious name to protect the real leaders' identities. The name Luddites has stuck to any group who resists productivity investments out of fear that their old jobs will be lost.

Lost jobs are highly visible. But invisible advantages occur when productivity is improved. First, more goods are available, and the price is likely to go down. In the case of the English weaving industry, industrialization benefited everyone who bought woven goods. Prices for woven goods fell, consumers wanted more, and people who previously could not afford woven goods became new consumers.

The American labor union movement has been treating Wal-Mart as a threat to workers. Wal-Mart has no unions, many part-time workers, and offers limited health benefits compared to unionized retailers. Wal-Mart has low prices, too—not just because of its lower labor costs but because it uses computing, telecommunications, and worldwide transportation to do a better job of finding the cheapest sources of goods. In California in 2003, unionized workers at three supermarket chains went on strike, not for higher wages but for increased job security because Wal-Mart was opening nonunion grocery stores in the area and competing with the strikers' employers. It was an odd strategy for unions to spend a half-year weakening unionized employers who were about to face a strong competitive challenge, but union leaders could not think of anything else to do. They also admitted that their striking members were shopping at Wal-Mart to save money, but they could not think how to deal with that either. The union members saw the advantage of low prices more clearly than the advantage of controlling the market.

The size of every industry mechanized during the Industrial Revolution, from weaving to retailing, has expanded beyond anyone's imagination—over and over again, greeted with the same technophobic reaction each time. After the Luddite reaction failed, the English textile industry went from about 8,000 people employed in 1771 to 320,000 people working in mills 27 years later.

Many of the people newly employed in the industrial economy were leaving subsistence farming and sharecropping. They were making their first appearance in the cash economy. They were becoming consumers of woven goods and many other industrial products, and their incomes were being multiplied into the wages and profits of others. Because England rejected the Luddites and industrialized—painfully but successfully—the country became the wealthiest nation on earth. Other nations in Europe and North America and Japan followed the English example. Wealth trickled down from the capitalists to every corner of society.

Western Europe, North America, and Japan, which have completed the journey of industrialization, are now creating a new economic system, known as globalization. Today, the same kind of industrial revolution is taking hold in China, India, and other parts of Asia, with much the same results.

The Power of Capital

As the U.S. leads the world in the transformation from a manufacturing economy to a service economy, it must continue to lead the world in productivity gains. Only the application of capital can give the workers better tools. Only the additional output made possible by the intelligent application of capital can continue to free more people from the factory floor without reducing production.

A hundred years ago, 40 percent of American workers toiled on farms to feed themselves and create a surplus that would feed the rest of the country. An economic revolution invested capital to mechanize farming. Most manual laborers were no longer needed. That pushed many Americans off farms and into factories, where their labor produced much more value. The remaining farmers, now using machines for almost everything to be done on much larger farms, were also far more productive For years now, another painful economic revolution has been automating factories and pushing those farmers' descendants out of manufacturing and into shops, delivery trucks, and offices, where their labor in services creates more value.

Economic efficiency requires that workers be motivated to find their most productive roles in the economy. Because a higher wage is one of the best motivators, economic efficiency virtually demands that workers be paid according to their productivity.

Few people recognize, however, that labor productivity is not a measure of workers' skill but a measure of the effectiveness of capital. Take two destitute persons digging a hole with their hands. Imagine that a capitalist—an owner of tools—gives a shovel to one of these hole-diggers. Compare the productivity of the digger with a shovel to the digger who uses only his hands. The capitalist who owns the shovel has made one worker more productive than the other. If they are paid according to their production, they face enormous income inequality. The one still digging with his hands faces a tremendous incentive to find a capitalist who will provide him with a shovel.

If digging holes has a marketable value, the worker with the shovel will shortly earn enough to pay a return on the capitalist's investment, who will buy another shovel and similarly equip the other hole-digger.

If hole-diggers and shovel-providing capitalists seem too simple to explain today's economy, consider this: Workers who use computers earn a 10 to 15 percent premium over the pay of workers with similar jobs whose employers do not provide them with computers. In many workplaces, the wage difference is 100 percent—applicants don't get jobs without computer skills.

Such income inequality is a sign of economic health.

The principal factor distinguishing high-paid labor from low-paid labor is productivity, and productivity is the product of investment. High-paid labor always involves labor of the mind, nowadays assisted by computer, which organizes and motivates the labor of muscles and machines.

One artisan could make a wagon for a farmer or a carriage for a wealthy man, but a thousand artisans cannot make a thousand Fords or Jaguars. They cannot make even one automobile unless they are properly organized and trained and given the proper tools. Financiers and managers turn blacksmiths and carpenters into assembly-line workers, increasing their productivity so much that the workers can afford automobiles.

Henry Ford provides the classic example. Between 1908 and 1913, Ford and his associates worked out better ways to build the Model T. Instead of assigning crews to build each car in a fixed location and bringing parts to them, they adopted the idea of assembling the car in motion, moving the car along a succession of stations, each equipped with appropriate parts and workers skilled at installing them. Likewise, large subassemblies moved on assembly lines of their own to meet the chassis. (This was Adam Smith's division of labor evolved from pins to large machines.)

At a new factory in Highland Park, Michigan, Ford operated his first power-driven assembly line in 1913. By the next year, the factory could make a Model T in 93 minutes, compared to production in a static factory that took 728 minutes. In 1914, Ford employed 13,000 workers to make 260,720 cars. All other companies in the car industry combined made 286,770 cars by the labor of 66,350 workers.

With that kind of productivity increase, it's little wonder that Ford could pay his workers $5 a day, twice the going rate in the Detroit area. The high pay reflected the value produced in his factories—he shared the productivity of his capital with the workers he had made more productive. Naturally, he was criticized. "I have heard it said, in fact, I believe it's quite a current thought, that we have taken skill out of work," he said in his 1922 autobiography, *My Life and Work*. "We have not. We have put a higher skill into planning, management, and tool building, and the results of that skill are enjoyed by the man who is not skilled."

The high pay also reflected a reality of that kind of labor. It was tedious and boring. Turnover was high and training was costly. In 1913, Ford had to hire 963 workers for every 100 needed. Ford's solution, the $5 day, was national news. He was called a fool and worse; there were predictions that the company would go bankrupt. Ford, however, reasoned that he could avoid enough of the cost of training new workers so that he could afford to pay the staff more, and that a well-paid work force would willingly follow instructions when presented with new, more efficient ways of doing jobs. Between 1914 and 1916, Ford Motor Co. profits doubled, from $30 million to $60 million.

"The payment of $5 a day for an eight-hour day was one of the finest cost-cutting moves we ever made," he said.

Ford also shared the productivity gain with his customers, cutting the price of Model Ts over and over again. The $825 car eventually sold for $275. The low price and the high wage even pushed his own workers into the class of people who could afford cars. Eventually they could even become investors.

Such things still happen in the modern globalizing world. In the 1970s the Indian auto industry, thoroughly protected behind trade barriers, was about 10 percent as productive as the Japanese auto industry. The Indian government experimented with a policy change in 1983 and permitted a Japanese company to build a car plant in a joint venture with an Indian company. The new plant was five times as productive as the other Indian plants, using local workers and materials sourced under the same conditions as the other Indian plants. The joint venture grew, prices of cars fell, and more Indian car companies learned to increase productivity. The lesson was clear: The working people of India benefited from importing Japanese capital and know-how.

The Wage Gap

In the U.S., high returns to high productivity usually lie obscured by statistics about the gap between the wages of workers who have not completed high school and workers who have completed college. As recently as the 1970s, a high-school diploma was a reasonable insurance policy against poverty, but its protective power is falling. Among white men, 93 percent of high-school graduates earned more than the poverty line in the 1970s, as did 84 percent of black male high-school graduates. Nowadays, the proportion of high-school graduates likely to earn more than a poverty-level income is 88 percent for white men and 75 percent for black men. This may have something to do with the declining quality of a high-school education—especially the high-school education in cities—but it also involves the declining power of a good high-school education to prepare a person for work in the twenty-first century.

There is a substantial college premium in the United States. Lifetime incomes of college graduates are about 50 percent greater than those of high school graduates, and the gap is increasing. Most of the entry-level jobs on the fast track to big salaries require a college degree. The BA or the BS is taken as evidence that the applicant has mental discipline and an ability to learn, even if the college grad never studied any skill related to the job on offer.

Instead of bemoaning such income and education gaps, we should be making sure they are well understood. We have universal access to higher education. All Americans should understand that they will be repaid for the time, effort, and financial sacrifice necessary to complete college because there is such an ample return on investment. Capital is also abundant. Most educated people have little trouble finding jobs that suit their skills. The obstacles are cultural. The important issue is to make the payoff more obvious and attractive than fantasies such as winning the lottery or playing in the National Football League.

America has completed the long effort to tear down barriers to entry into better-paying fields. Businesses in competitive industries cannot afford to exclude workers because of bias or bigotry. Weaker unions no longer can exclude minorities and women from whole industries. Where craft-union membership once helped plumbers and carpenters pass their trades down from father to son, now computer-aided design tools help anyone's son or daughter learn a trade.

Competitive financial institutions now bid for high-powered MBAs and lawyers instead of conferring partnerships on the graduates of the Ivy League. And those same banks place capital where it will earn the most. Those who would start businesses need a sound business plan, rather than a sound pedigree to attract capital.

Nowadays skill in the workplace gets a greater reward. Unions no longer command top dollar for unskilled workers in huge manufacturing industries. In the whole economy, more demand exists for workers who gather, analyze, and pass on information, and such workers are more productive than they used to be.

High productivity generates high profits, and high profits lead quickly to unequal distributions of wealth and income that favor the owners of capital. This is not only inevitable, but because of the 80-20 rule, it is desirable. "To get rich is glorious," as Deng Xiaoping said in putting China on the path to rapid growth. Inequality, even the wretched excess of inherited wealth, is a powerful teacher. Those who best learn the lesson of inequality will be most motivated to overcome it. Half of the growth of U.S. inequality in the past 25 years occurred within education groups. Inequality also has been driven by the gains of some college graduates relative to others. More people are going to college just to get the necessities of writing, history, geography, and math that students 50 years ago acquired with their high-school educations. A graduate degree has become the signal of superior effort and knowledge that a bachelor's degree once transmitted, and before that, a high school diploma certified. It is no coincidence that high-school graduation rates have risen from 10 percent of the population of 18-year-olds to about 70 percent at the same time that the value of a high-school diploma has fallen in the marketplace. What is not scarce is not valued; what is not difficult to obtain is not valued.

The concentration of income from investments is another important cause of inequality. Capital gains and interest income are distributed to the owners of investments, who are concentrated at the upper end of the income scale. More than half of all capital income went to the top 1 percent of American income earners.

Investments in human capital pay off just as other investments do. Increased ordinary incomes for college and graduate educations are also returns on capital investments. An important question is why the response to this personal investment incentive is not greater than it is. About 30 percent of students drop out before graduating from high school. If they do not believe this reduces their future prospects, they must believe they never had any prospects. The primary education system failed such students. They did not acquire the basic knowledge and the study skills necessary to get through high school, so going to college is not a choice but an impossibility.

Fixing elementary public education, which is failing so many children in cities and poor rural areas and fails many even in wealthier suburbs, is no simple task. It requires money, high standards, and extra effort in and out of school by teachers and parents. But criticizing American income inequality is not going to help, nor is taxing the rich and subsidizing the poor. That amounts to a tax penalty for success and a subsidy for failure.

Unequal Wealth Rises Anyway

American poverty isn't what it used to be, for which all Americans should be thankful. The 12.3 percent of Americans who were officially designated as poor in 2006 lived better than the poor people of 20 years ago, 50 years ago, or 100 years ago. Economists who analyze poverty issues call this the "income elasticity of the poverty line." By any title, what it means is that somebody has remembered to ask, "Poor as compared to what?"

Because the wealth of the nation rises continually and because scientists, engineers, and manufacturers are continually providing more and better goods, the average American standard of living rises accordingly. Americans whose standard of living does not rise as fast as the average fall toward poverty compared to the average. And those poor people whose standard of living rises with the average remain poor by comparison—but they have more stuff.

Two centuries ago, even a wealthy man such as George Washington did not have central heating. A hundred years ago, the indoor toilet, the electric light, and the telephone were found only in a few homes that could afford to install them. These conveniences became middle-class necessities and now are commonplace items in virtually every American home, even the poorest.

Today's poor also have a better social safety net. Dust Bowl refugees from the 1930s had next to nothing when their farms stopped producing and little in the way of local charity to fall back on because their neighbors were also hard up. Unemployed factory workers may have had more resources, such as shoes and overcoats, but they had more expenses, too. Life on "relief," or in one of the Depression-era tent cities for the dispossessed called Hoovervilles, seems shocking today because all of us, including the poor, have come so far.

The Census Bureau says that national income is rising faster than the reported poverty line. Poverty income buys more than it did 10 years ago. On the other hand, people with a poverty income are further behind the average and much further behind the people with high incomes than they used to be.

The challenge for citizens who pay the bills for poverty programs is to discern whether the rising living standard of the nation's poorest people is good news—the poor are better off than those who were in their plight in the old days—or bad news—the poor are on the wrong side of a widening income gap.

Those who say that the widening income gap is bad news rarely acknowledge the improving general standard of living. It is true that "a rising tide lifts all the boats" and that "trickle-down economics" is a blessing, not a curse.

The Highest Return on Investment

"The social object of skilled investment should be to defeat the dark forces of time and ignorance which envelop our future," said John Maynard Keynes, who surpassed his skills as an economic analyst with his skills as an investor.

Investment seeks the highest return, which means that the aim of investment is to put capital to work, enhancing the productivity of ordinary labor. Returns on investment can be reinvested, and this compounds the returns on the original principal. Capital formation—the accumulation of wealth—must be the first concern for a country interested in growth through investment. We cannot continue to invest in America if all we do is borrow the capital by running up the national debt. With our national debt approaching $10 trillion, we have run through our capital, our children's capital, foreign savers' capital, and their children's capital. We should take a break. We should have a national economic summit to discuss realistic plans to reduce the national debt, using taxes on consumption and sweeping spending cuts across every sector of the federal budget—from Social Security to farm subsidies to the American defense of Europe.

Some say deficit spending is a good cure for recession. But if it works, it will be adopted as a good cure for slow growth, and if the economy speeds up a little more, deficit spending will seem to be a good cure for moderate growth. Better things than growth exist, if that growth is merely borrowed from future earnings. Pumped-up growth gives us enormous deficits and makes us dependent on somebody else's capital accumulations, instead of pushing us to create our own capital out of our own profits.

When some economists talk about investment, they mean public investment, and their purpose is usually to stimulate the economy. They are not satisfied with the inclinations of private investors, who usually are somewhat more risk averse. After all, private investors have to safeguard their own money; governments are investing tax money. Just as economists have promoted consumption in the aggregate—of any kind by anyone for any reason—they promote investment without much concern for the type of investment or its profitability. The object is to goose the economy, not to preserve capital or make a return on investment.

A favorite tool of such economists is the investment tax credit, a tax break for the purchase of new equipment that has been enacted and repealed in the U.S. Congress three times in the past 30 years without any discernible effect on productivity or prosperity. That economists would wish to bring the credit back and add a new credit for the purchase of real estate suggests that the fall in property values after 2006 reached the faculty houses that surround the groves of academe.

Another perennial favorite with some economists is a big federal investment in public infrastructure under the administration of the states—highways, bridges, railroads, ports, airfields, sports stadiums, even private factories. The states, you see, have deferred many worthwhile capital projects, which they would no doubt reinstate if the money were available. The money would be available if the political support were available. A state can raise taxes, cut other spending, or even borrow, if its citizens believe that an adequate return on investment will result. A substantial number of citizens, however, prefer that their states do less and tax less. If they are allowed to make their own choices with their own money, many choose new cars over a tax to build new highways, at least until congestion gets intolerable.

That's the time to tax and invest. Sure, we would all like free money for our schools, highways, and hospitals. But money isn't free, even when Uncle Sam borrows it to bestow on states, which then spend it as if it were free money.

The test of a national economic policy should be whether we wish to raise real money from real lenders and real taxpayers because we anticipate real returns on our investments. Anybody can throw money at schools; it's far harder to find evidence that adding more classrooms to reduce class sizes really produces better-educated students. Anybody can throw money at highways; it's far harder to tell the rural constituency that the only reason a rural county needs a six-lane highway is to bring developers out to wave money under the noses of a few farmers.

The profit test should also be the test of a private investment strategy, but it's no easier to put into practice. Real-estate interests would do anything to bring back easy mortgages. The aerospace industry longs for generous research contracts. Steel makers and car companies want their investments sheltered under protection from foreign competition.

Everybody, even people who built businesses and bought homes on easy credit, bemoans the scarcity of capital. But the availability of capital is controlled by investors' enthusiasm, and fear, which run in cycles. Sometimes too much capital exists relative to the number of sound investments. Every investment cycle reaches this phase: In the past it has produced financing for dozens of personal-computer companies, each seeking 10 percent of the market, and for hundreds of biotech companies, each promising a potential cure for the same dozen diseases. Microchips, calculators, disc drives, supercomputers—venture capitalists are ready to support any idea twice over, and investment bankers are ready to bring the public in when the venture partners want to cash out. Money for housing and money for mortgages is sometimes so easy to obtain that it leads to excessive house prices.

Other times, investors demand high interest rates, even for secure investments. They won't put their money into the next new thing or even into the same old things. They won't buy houses because they think the price can only go down.

Neither phase lasts forever. If capital weren't scarce in the fearful phase, there would be few investment profits and capitalism couldn't exist. Those investments that succeed create fresh capital. But if too many investments succeed, capital is abundant, and it's scattered over many more investments, each of which seems a sure thing. Remember the dot-com bubble? Of course, risk always turns out to be the greatest when it appears to be the least. Capitalism works because of scarcity and risk. The market allocates scarce capital to competing risky investment opportunities and rewards the wisest and the luckiest investors.

Creative Disorder

Markets must be free to produce the most efficient distribution of goods and services. But free markets full of free people are chaotic and unpredictable. Orderly trading suddenly becomes disorderly, even panicky, on the upside or the downside. Every now and then, market prices rise rapidly, usually in expectation of huge profits from some new technology or economic development. In the U.S., bubbles have occurred for telegraphy, railroads, electricity, radio, aircraft, casinos, computers, and the Internet, to name a few, and local and national real-estate bubbles have occurred once a generation at least. All of them came to bad ends—bankruptcies for some companies and big losses for some unwary investors.

Bubbles also brought capital to new industries and quickly financed the creation of infrastructures that lasted for generations. Examples include the railroad bubble, radio bubble, and broadband Internet bubble. Just because a boom is often followed by a bust doesn't mean the boom was bad for the nation.

At any time, we may be riding the crest of a wave that shortly will break upon the beach and crush us—not just in the stock market but in the markets for homes and other property. On the upswing, participants in a speculative bubble are getting richer. As John Kenneth Galbraith said, "No one wishes to believe that this is fortuitous or undeserved; all wish to think that it is the result of their own superior insight or intuition."

Galbraith, however, was convinced that markets' characteristic swings from boom to bust are undesirable. As he put it, "Recurrent descent into insanity is not a wholly attractive feature of capitalism."

But it is a very important feature of capitalism. Waves of boom and bust have washed over the most productive economies in history, especially the American economy. They have broken down entrenched financial power and unleashed repressed creativity with the power of cheap profits, cheap labor, and cheap materials. Though booms may lead to busts, busts create the conditions for future booms.

The government's job is to stay out of the way of natural economic cycles and let markets work. When governments fight economic cycles, they usually make them worse.

Capitalism fosters freedom of action, ideally freedom of individuals to act in the market with other individuals, lobbying and bribing to obtain favorable treatment for their business endeavors. People may work together in limited ways to ensure that the market is fair in addition to free, but capitalists—from experience—view government with suspicion and caution.

Capitalists should work to constrict the power of government. Unfortunately, real capitalists all too often attempt to use the power of government to their advantage, lobbying and bribing to obtain favorable treatment for their business endeavors. No government can be entirely free of corruption; people aren't that good. Only a government of limited powers derived from the consent of the governed can resist the temptation to absolute corruption because it has been foreclosed from absolute power.

Summary

Adam Smith proposed a fundamental principle of liberty: "Every man, as long as he does not violate the laws of justice, is left perfectly free to pursue his own interest his own way."

He declared that people competing with their industry and their capital would arrange society better than any sovereign, who could not possibly know enough about the affairs of his kingdom's people to organize their activities in the directions most beneficial to society. The famous "invisible hand" of self-interest causes individuals "without knowing it [to] advance the interest of the society."

To some, Adam Smith's invisible hand is as immaterial and unlikely as Karl Marx's "withering away" of the state is to others. But the division of labor and wealth—and the invisible hand that divides wealth according to the productivity of individuals—are the fundamental engine of the modern capitalist economy.

Reading Further

If this book has inspired you to read more about economics, some suggestions follow.

Periodicals

Barron's National Business and Financial Weekly

The Wall Street Journal

The New York Times

The Economist

The Financial Times

Books

Payback: Reaping the Rewards of Innovation by James P. Andrew and Harold L. Sirkin

Good Capitalism, Bad Capitalism by William J. Baumol, Robert E. Litan, and Carl Schramm

The Modern Corporation and Private Property by Adolf Berle and Gardiner Means

Against the Gods: The Remarkable Story of Risk by Peter Bernstein

The Birth of Plenty by William Bernstein

The J Curve by Ian Bremmer

New Ideas from Dead Economists by Todd G. Buchholz

The Visible Hand by Alfred D. Chandler

The Innovator's Dilemma by Clayton M. Christensen

The Rich and How They Got That Way by Cynthia Crossen

Collapse and Guns and Germs and Steel by Jared Diamond

Economics for Dummies by Sean Masaki Flynn

America Works by Richard Freeman

The Myth of the Robber Barrons by Burton W. Folsom Jr.

Hidden Order: The Economics of Everyday Life
by David Friedman

Capitalism and Freedom, Free to Choose, and *Money Mischief*
by Milton Friedman

The Age of the Economist by Daniel R. Fusfeld

The Capitalist Philosophers by Andrea Gabor

Wealth & Poverty by George Gilder

An Empire of Wealth and *The Scarlet Woman of Wall Street*
by John Steele Gordon

Security Analysis by Benjamin Graham and David L. Dodd

Money of the Mind by James Grant

One World, Ready or Not by William Greider

The Undercover Economist by Tim Harford

Economics in One Lesson by Henry Hazlitt

The Nature and Logic of Capitalism and *The Worldly
Philosophers* by Robert Heilbroner

The Robber Barons by Matthew Josephson

Reviving the Invisible Hand by Deepak Lal

The Armchair Economist by Steven E. Landsburg

Freakonomics by Steven D. Levitt and Stephen J. Dubner

Are the Rich Necessary? by Hunter Lewis

Freedomnomics by John R. Lott Jr.

The Bankers, The Fate of the Dollar, and *The Fed* by Martin Mayer

The Economics of Public Issues by Roger LeRoy Miller, Daniel K. Benjamin, and Douglass C. North

Money, Method and the Market Process, Selected Essays by Ludwig von Mises

The Masters of Capital by John Moody

On The Wealth of Nations by P.J. O'Rourke

FDR's Folly by Jim Powell

They Told Barron and *More They Told Barron* edited by Arthur Pound and Samuel Taylor Moore

The Mind and the Market by Jerry Z. Muller

The Politically Incorrect Guide to Capitalism by Robert P. Murphy

In Search of Excellence by Thomas J. Peters and Robert H. Waterman Jr.

The Competitive Advantage of Nations by Michael E. Porter

The Fortune at the Bottom of the Pyramid by C.K. Prahalad

Saving Capitalism from the Capitalists Raghuram G. Rajan and Luigi Zingales

The Antitrust Religion by Edwin S. Rockefeller

The Good Life and Its Discontents by Robert J. Samuelson

The Forgotten Man and *The Greedy Hand* by Amity Schlaes

The Entrepreneurial Imperative by Carl J. Schramm

Capitalism, Socialism and Democracy by Joseph A. Schumpeter

The Wealth of Nations by Adam Smith

Paper Money by Adam Smith [George Goodman]

The Worldly Economists by Robert Sobel

The Other Path and *The Mystery of Capital*
by Hernando de Soto

Morgan: American Financier by Jean Strouse

Taking Sides: Clashing Views on Controversial Economic Issues
by Thomas R. Swartz and Frank J. Bonello

A Thousand Barrels a Second by Peter Tertzakian

The Way the World Works by Jude Wanniski

The Merchant of Power by John F. Wasik

Government Failure versus Market Failure by Clifford Winston

Maestro by Bob Woodward

INDEX

A

absolute advantage, 62

affordable health care versus universal health care versus high-quality health care, 131-132

agriculture industry, protectionism of, 53

alternative minimum tax (AMT), 103

American Medical Association, 133

American party, 66

amnesty for illegal immigrants, 68, 78

AMT (alternative minimum tax), 103

antitrust legislation, 122-127

appliances, tax credits for energy efficiency, 11

appraisers, role in real-estate bubble, 174

Arizona example (illegal immigration legislation), 70-73

assimilation of ethnic minorities, 76

atomic bombs, nuclear power versus, 14

Atomic Energy Commission, 15

automobiles, tax credits for energy efficiency, 12

B

baby boomers, effect on national economy, 161-165

Babylonian Code of Hammurabi, 121

birth rates, 88

Bismarck, Otto von, 154

Bloomberg, Michael, 108-110

borrowers, role in real-estate bubble, 174

Bradford, Scott, 56

British coal supply example, 19-20

British colonial power, free trade and, 44

brokers, role in real-estate bubble, 174

Burr, Aaron, 46

Bush, George W., 10, 94-95, 97-98, 119, 162, 172

C

California
  development in, 42
  electricity crisis, 122

Canadian lumber industry example (restraint of trade), 47-48

unilateral free trade, 52
  in United States, history of, 43-47
French mercantile system, 60-62
Friedman, Milton, 182
fuel, 13
Fuller, Ida Mae, 150
funding shortfalls in Social Security
  and Medicare, 157-161

G

Galbraith, John Kenneth, 116, 199
gasoline, price controls on, 13
Gates, Bill, 123
GDP
  energy consumption and, 4
  energy efficiency versus, 27
General Electric, 85
General Motors, 135
Generations X and Y, effect on
  national economy, 166-168
Gibbon, Edward, 104
Glendower, Owen, 176
global economy
  free trade benefits, 56-57
  free trade versus protectionism,
    49-55
  immigration, effect of, 75-76
global warming, 23
Gore, Al, 23
government regulation, 116
Great Depression, 179-180
greater fool theory, 171
Greenspan, Alan, 153, 172, 183
Grieco, Paul, 56
growth limits in ecosystem, 35-36
guest-worker programs, 67, 78

H

Hamilton, Alexander, 45-46
Hammurabi, code of, 121
Hardin, Garrett, 39
Hayek, Friedrich A., 31
health care, 140
  cost per capita, 137-138
  rising cost of, 139-140
health care system
  alternatives to current system,
    144-147
  reform efforts, list of, 133-137
  universal versus affordable versus
    high-quality, 131-132
health insurance
  alternatives to current system,
    144-147
  cost of, 142-143
  legislation concerning, 135-137
Henry IV, Part I (Shakespeare), 176
high-quality health care versus
  universal health care versus
  affordable health care, 131-132
history
  of free trade in United States, 43-47
  of immigration in United States,
    65-69
holding companies, 86
Holmes, Oliver Wendell Jr., 93
home ownership, tax benefits of, 169
Hong Kong, unilateral free trade
  in, 52
Hotspur, Henry, 176
housing bubble, 120, 169
Hubbert, M. King, 17
Huckabee, Mike, 105
Hufbauer, Gary, 56
Hume, David, 62